j599.5 Sattler, Helen
SAT   Roney.

        Whales, the nomads
          of the sea

DEC 7 1988

    $14.00   f p

DATE			
SEP 2 7 1989	1316	FEB. 2 1995	1476
DEC 1 3 1989	1317	MAR 2 1995	1476
		SEP. 2 0 1995	1575
JUL 5 1990	1311	FEB. 8 1996	1505
		FEB. 2 1 1996	1546
SEP 19 1990	1394	OCT. 2 3 1996	1554
JUN. 1 1 1992	1470	JAN. 2 9 1997	1546
DEC. 9 1992	1435	APR. 1 0 1997	1547
SEP. 1 1993	1500	JUN. 1 1 1997	1613
OCT. 2 1 1993	1500	FEB. 2 5 1998	1653
AUG. 1 7 1994	153	SEP 0 4 2003	1777
JAN. 2 6 1995	1476	MAR 1 1 2004	1762

© THE BAKER & TAYLOR CO.

WHALES,
the Nomads of the Sea

boy riding a dolphin

WHALES,
the Nomads of the Sea

by Helen Roney Sattler

illustrated by Jean Day Zallinger

LOTHROP, LEE & SHEPARD BOOKS | NEW YORK

ACKNOWLEDGMENTS

With special thanks to Dr. William Evans, Director of Hubbs–Sea World Research Institute, who read the manuscript and checked the illustrations for accuracy. In addition to those cited in the "For Further Reading" section, I am indebted to the following writers and scientists for information gleaned from their papers and articles: Richard H. Backus, Lawrence Barnes, Ben Bennett, Malcolm Clarke, Sylvia Earle, William J. L. Felts, Phillip Gingerich, William Graves, James Gray, F. W. de Haan, Donald Heintzelman, John Kanwisher, Lawrence Kruger, Thomas Lang, Jon Lien, John Lilly, L. Harrison Matthews, Faith McNulty, Kenneth Norris, Peter E. Purves, D. A. Parry, John Reynolds III, Steven L. Swartz, Margaret Tavolga, W. H. Dudok Van Heel, and Paul D. White.

Library of Congress Cataloging in Publication Data
Sattler, Helen Roney.   Whales, the nomads of the sea.
Bibliography: p. Includes index. Summary: Discusses the physical characteristics, habits, natural environment, and relationship to human beings of whales and dolphins. Includes a glossary giving the popular and scientific name of each species and details of their size and appearance. 1. Cetacea—Juvenile literature. 2. Whales—Juvenile literature. 3. Dolphins—Juvenile literature. [1. Whales. 2. Dolphins] I. Zallinger, Jean, ill. II. Title.
QL737.C4S27   1987   599.5   86–10397
ISBN 0–688–05587–7

DESIGNED BY SYLVIA FREZZOLINI

Dedicated to
the passengers and crew
of the *Tradition*

Contents

gray whale (*E. robustus*) spyhopping

Chapter 1

Friendly Giants

"Spout at two o'clock," called the captain of our small ship.

Everyone rushed to the bow-rail, eager to catch a glimpse of live whales. Whales were spouting all around us.

Suddenly a forty-ton gray whale leaped into the air and fell back into the water with a tremendous splash. Others poked their heads above the waves and eyed us as we passed. I wondered who was watching whom. Was it possible that whales were as fascinated with humans as we were with them?

People have been fascinated by whales for thousands of years. These great animals live in a world very alien to our own. Many scientists have spent their lives studying them, yet we still don't know much about these incredible creatures that roam the unseen highways that crisscross our oceans.

Whales are hard to get to know. They can't survive on land, and we can't live in the ocean. A few smaller whales have been studied in aquariums, but bigger whales—those known as the great whales—are too large, and too expensive to feed, to be studied in captivity for long.

One of the most astonishing facts about whales is their apparent interest in humans. Many smaller ones seem to enjoy human company. In captivity they eagerly engage in experiments and seem to cooperate more for approval than for reward. Throughout the ages numerous stories have been told of wild dolphins swimming with children or rescuing people at sea.

Not long ago a dolphin saved the life of an eleven-year-old boy who had been surfing near the shore of an island in the Indian Ocean when a strong wave swept him out to sea. He could see sharks all around and was frightened until a dolphin came and chased the sharks away. The dolphin stayed with the boy until he was rescued four hours later. In the past few years there have been reports of large whales, too, that have acted friendly toward people.

Until quite recently all that was known about large whales came from studying the carcasses of harpooned or beached whales. There is little resemblance between the bloated body of a dead whale and the supple, majestic body of a great whale breaching (leaping into the air) or swimming underwater.

Today scientists know of several places where they can study whales in their natural habitat. One of these places is San Ignacio Lagoon of Baja California. Every winter hundreds of gray whales go there to mate and have their babies. The lagoon is a good place to become acquainted with these fascinating nomads, so that is where I went to meet a whale face to face.

I soon discovered that not much can be learned about the life of a whale from the deck of a ship. As exciting as our first sight of a great whale was, we saw very little of the actual animals the first morning. We barely had time to catch a glimpse of them as the great creatures surfaced for a breath of air, then arched their backs and dived beneath the waters of the lagoon.

Some of us left the ship and boarded inflatable skiffs to search for a friendly gray whale. At first the whales would not let us come near them.

But every few minutes they poked their heads out of the water and looked us over. Early whalers called this spyhopping.

After a while a forty-five-foot female started following us. Soon she was joined by two younger whales. They seemed to be interested in our skiff. They came nearer and hung in the water with their flukes down. Their huge snouts towered ten feet above the surface as they watched us with their cantaloupe-sized eyes.

Then one of them came over and nudged our skiff with its head. After that the three whales began to play with us and let us pet them. They seemed to like being rubbed on the snout. Their skin felt like a wet inner tube.

The big female, who was three times as long as our skiff, swam under us and lifted the skiff with her head. She took us for a short ride, then let us down.

Sometimes the whales blew bubbles all around us and under our skiff. The air came out of their blowholes with such force, it felt as if someone were hitting the bottom of the boat with rocks. One whale swam close and, while still a few inches underwater, blasted air out of its blowholes, giving us a cold shower. I think it liked to hear us scream.

We could tell where the whales were, even when they were completely submerged. Each time a whale beat its tail, a column of water rose to the top and left a smooth patch on the surface. Scientists call these spots footprints.

One whale played with us for three hours. When it was time for us to go back to our ship, it didn't want us to leave. It followed us all the way back.

gray whale

gray whale spyhopping

gray whale

13

I couldn't believe it! These forty-ton whales were incredibly strong and easily could have smashed our small skiff with one whack of their great tails or upset us by ramming the boat with their heads. But they didn't. Controlling their enormous bodies and great flukes, they moved as easily and gracefully as ballerinas.

Wild deer and raccoons may be coaxed to come close to people if they are offered something to eat. But these whales did not come to us for food. They came to play with us, just as we might play with a kitten. After looking a gray whale in the eye, I was eager to learn more about these incredible animals.

Chapter 2

Amazing Mammals

WHALES ARE MAMMALS. THOUGH THEY LIVE IN THE SEA LIKE FISH, THEY are not fish. Whales are warm-blooded and maintain an average body temperature of about 96.8 degrees (close to that of humans), regardless of the temperature of the water around them. They have lungs and must breathe air just as humans must. Like all mammals, they have hair at some stage of their lives, and they give birth to live young, which are fed milk from the mother's body. Also, like all other mammals, they have four-chambered hearts.

A great whale's heart is enormous—250 pounds in a gray whale. However, when compared to the size of the animal, a whale's heart takes up no more space than a cat's heart. A whale's heart beats very slowly; the larger the animal, the slower the heartbeat. A sparrow's heart beats a thousand times a minute, the human heart beats about seventy-five times a minute, but a gray whale's heart beats only nine times a minute.

Slowing of the heartbeat is only one of the ways in which these mammals changed in order to live in the sea. Scientists believe that the ancestors of whales lived on land. More than sixty million years ago they probably had nostrils at the end of their snouts, and four short legs, and they may have been covered with fur like other mammals.

Scientists have found fossils of a six-foot fish-eating land animal, which they think may have been an ancestor of the whale. This creature was closely related to the ancestors of modern hoofed animals. Blood tests of today's whales show that they are more closely related to cows, goats, camels, and elephants than to any other living animal.

eye of a gray whale

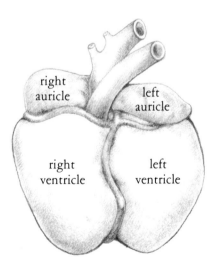

shape of great whale's heart

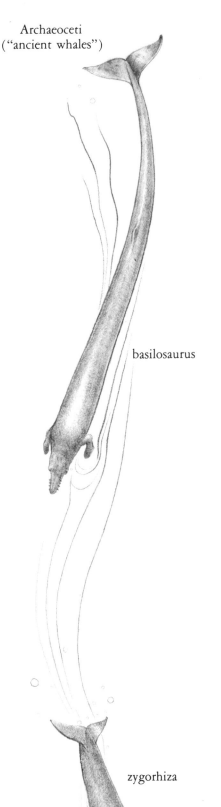

Archaeoceti
("ancient whales")

basilosaurus

zygorhiza

blowhole

Whale ancestors probably lived near the sea. Like hippopotamuses, they may have spent much of the day in shallow water near the shore searching for food. Gradually they had to go farther from shore and stay longer in the water to find food or escape predators. Finally the survivors (those that didn't drown) were spending all of their time in the water.

Whales with the most streamlined bodies were more efficient swimmers, so they survived and bore young that were better adapted to the watery environment. Slowly, over millions of years, their forelegs became flippers. All parts that interfered with smooth passage through water gradually disappeared. Thick layers of fat or blubber kept them warm better than hair. Therefore hair, except for a few bristles on the head and chin, disappeared. Ear flaps and hind legs vanished. The tail developed broad flukes. The nostrils moved from the tip of the snout to the top of the head, so the whale could breathe while floating. Eventually, whales could no longer live on land, even for a short period. They no longer needed to. They had become completely adapted for living in the sea.

Modern whales still show indications of their land origins. Their flippers contain the same bones that all mammalian arms and hands do, and all whales still have traces of hip and leg bones buried in muscles below the spine. Buds of hind limbs can be seen in embryos (unborn babies), and occasionally a whale is born with tiny hind legs.

Scientists call whales cetaceans (see-TAY-shuns), which comes from *cetus,* the Latin word for whale. There are three major groups of whales: no two of them are any more closely related to each other than goats, sheep, and deer are. Only two of the major groups are living today, the Mysticeti (MISS-tuh-SEE-tee) or baleen whales, and the Odontoceti (o-DON-tuh-SEE-tee) or toothed whales. The third group, the Archaeoceti (ARE-keh-o-SEE-tee) or "ancient whales," is extinct.

The archaeocetes lived from 50 million to 25 million years ago. Though it was once thought that they all had long snakelike bodies, it is now known that some looked much like modern whales.

The mysticetes first appeared about 30 million years ago. They are the largest animals on earth, ranging from the size of an automobile to as long as three hook-and-ladder trucks placed end to end. *Mysticeti* means "mustached whales," referring to the horny plates of baleen (whalebone) in their mouths. The baleen is used to filter food from the sea. There are ten species of baleen whales. All have two blowholes.

The odontocetes appeared about the same time as the baleen whales. Most living whales are odontocetes. There are sixty-six species in this group, and they include the porpoises and dolphins. *Odontoceti* means "toothed whales," and all of these whales have teeth, although in some species the teeth are hidden in the gums. The number of visible teeth varies from 1 to 240. These whales have a single blowhole. Most have a melon (a large rounded mass of blubber) on top of their heads. The smallest odontocete is about as long as an average ten-year-old child is tall. The largest, the sperm whale, is longer than the largest semitrailer truck.

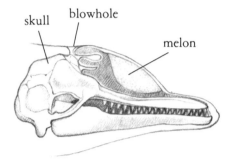

head of a porpoise (toothed whale)
cross section

skull   blowhole   melon

Usually when people hear the word *whale,* they think of a gigantic baleen whale or a sperm whale. But not all whales are huge. Whales come in many shapes and sizes. Of the seventy-six different species, no two are alike. More than half of the toothed whales are less than ten feet long.

Most baleen whales, however, are enormous. The fin whale may be eighty feet long (longer than a railroad passenger car) and weigh fifty tons. The gigantic blue whale, the largest animal that has ever lived, is one hundred feet long (as long as two diesel locomotives) and weighs up to two hundred tons (as much as thirty elephants). Some dinosaurs may have been as long, but none weighed anywhere near as much. The smallest mysticete, the pygmy right whale, weighs as much as an African elephant, which is the largest land animal alive today.

Whales can grow to be much larger than land animals because their bodies are supported by water. In water they are almost weightless. A land animal's legs could not support such great weight.

Thick layers of blubber or fat help whales float. They also insulate against heat loss. Whales that live in icy polar waters have thicker blubber than those of warmer oceans. A bowhead's blubber may be two feet thick. Blue whales may carry twenty tons of fat. In addition to being insulated with fat, whales keep warm by moving almost constantly.

Most whales have distinctive shapes—the right whales are shaped like tugboats, fin whales are cruiser-shaped, and sperm whales have submarine-like bodies. Their color doesn't vary as much as their shape and size. A few whales are all black or all white, but most are either black and white or some shade of gray (the blue whale is actually blue-gray). Those that feed on or near the surface have dark backs and light-colored bellies. This helps them blend in with their surroundings and makes it easier for them to

MYSTICETI

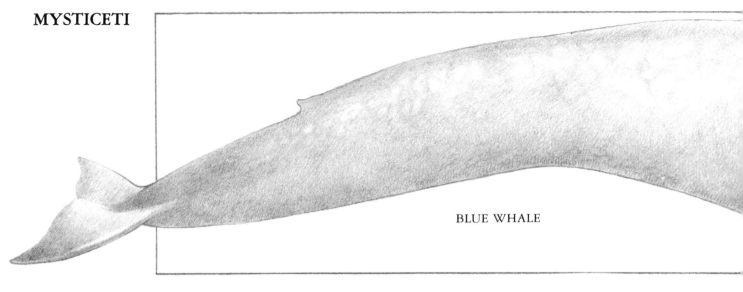

BLUE WHALE

ODONTOCETI

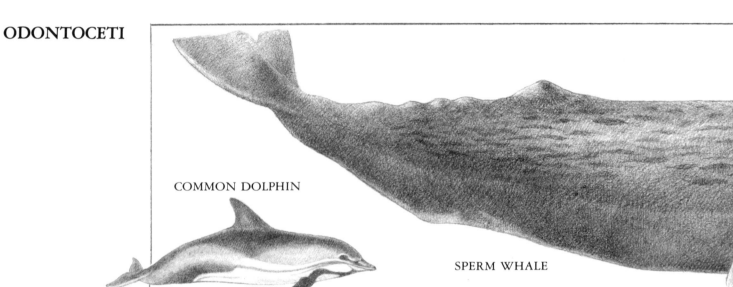

COMMON DOLPHIN

SPERM WHALE

**ANCIENT
CETACEA
(WHALES)**

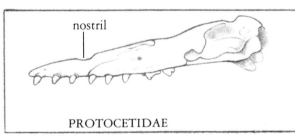

nostril

PROTOCETIDAE

nostril

DORUDONTIDAE

about 45 million years ago
middle Eocene

about 40 million years ago
late Eocene

**CREODONT
(PRESUMED
ANCESTOR
OF WHALES)**

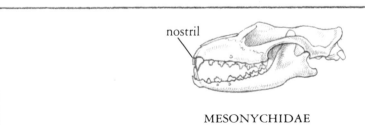

nostril

MESONYCHIDAE

about 50 million years ago

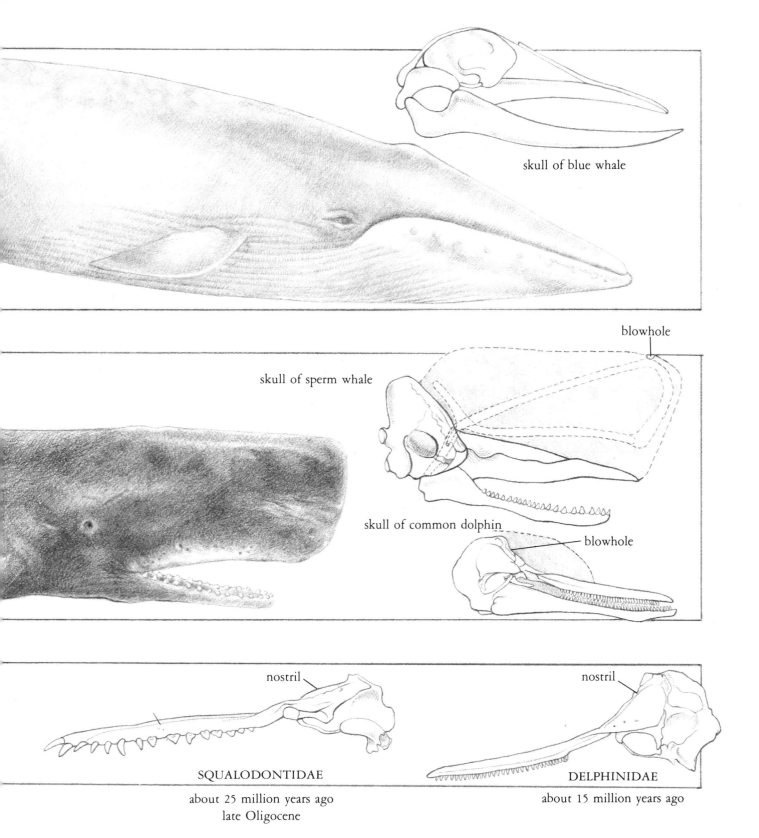

skull of blue whale

blowhole

skull of sperm whale

skull of common dolphin

blowhole

nostril

nostril

SQUALODONTIDAE

DELPHINIDAE

about 25 million years ago
late Oligocene

about 15 million years ago

FIFTY MILLION YEARS
OF WHALE DEVELOPMENT

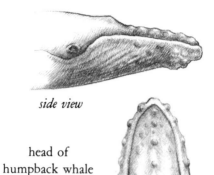

side view

head of
humpback whale
(baleen)

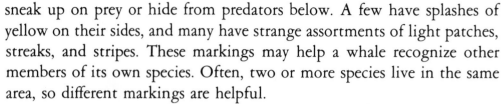

from belou

sneak up on prey or hide from predators below. A few have splashes of yellow on their sides, and many have strange assortments of light patches, streaks, and stripes. These markings may help a whale recognize other members of its own species. Often, two or more species live in the same area, so different markings are helpful.

Each species of whale has a different skull shape. Like most mammals, all whales have seven vertebrae in the neck. In most the vertebrae are very short, and in some they are fused together. A short neck makes the body more streamlined.

These streamlined nomads visit every ocean and sea in the world, and some dolphins even go into freshwater rivers and lakes. Yet many people have never seen a whale, because most whales live in the open sea. Whales roam vast areas, including the Antarctic oceans, where people seldom go. A few kinds are rarely seen by anyone. Some kinds have never been seen alive. It is possible that there are species of whales that no one has seen.

But this is changing rapidly. Today we know much more about whales than we did a few years ago. More and more whale-watching is being done, and scientists are learning ways to tell individual whales apart. This helps us to better understand how whales live.

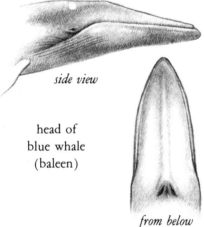
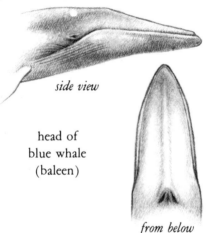

side view

head of
blue whale
(baleen)

from below

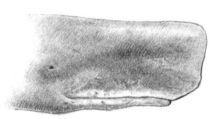

side view

side view

head of
Hubbs' beaked whale
(toothed), male
two teeth in lower jaw
one blowhole

side view

head of
right whale
(baleen)

from below

head of
sperm whale
(toothed)
one blowhole

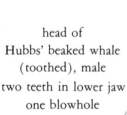

from below

from below

Chapter 3

Blowholes and Butterfly Flukes

spout of sperm whale
(*front view*)

spout of right whale
(*front view*)

spout of blue whale

spout of humpback whale

WHEN A GRAY WHALE SURFACES, ONLY THE TOP OF ITS HEAD AND A SMALL part of its back are visible. With a loud swoosh, a geyserlike spout of water shoots fifteen feet into the air. This is followed by a piercing whistle as the huge animal inhales through its two gaping eight-inch blowholes. It may blow five more times, then dive, its enormous flukes appearing briefly like a giant butterfly's wings. Ten minutes later it may surface two thousand feet away.

People who know whales can tell what kind of whale made the blow by the shape and height of the column of water. A sperm whale's spout slants forward and to the left, right whales have V-shaped spouts, and a humpback's is shaped like an upside-down pear. A blue whale's thirty-foot blow is cone-shaped.

The spout is formed when air from the lungs is expelled through the nostrils. A whale's nostrils are located in the blowholes (which may be rectangular, S-shaped, crescent-shaped, or crosswise slits) on top of its head. Gray whales are baleen whales and have two blowholes. Although toothed whales have only one blowhole, they have two nostrils and two air passages, the same as baleen whales and other mammals.

It was once thought that the spout was the moisture in warm air expelled from the lungs condensing when it hit cool air (like what happens to your breath on a cold day). But spouts are seen just as often at the equator as at the North Pole. And sometimes whales exhale without forming spouts. Scientists now think that the spout is a mixture of water

spout of
Hubbs' beaked whale

right whales (*E. glacialis*)

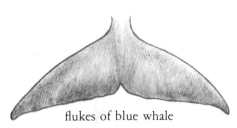

flukes of blue whale

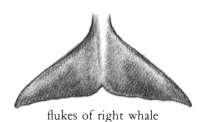

flukes of right whale

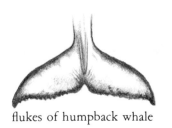

flukes of humpback whale

flukes of sperm whale

flukes of
Hubbs' beaked whale

droplets and exhaled air. Seawater collects in depressions around the blowholes. Air is expelled from the lungs so forcefully—at 120 miles per hour in a gray whale and up to 300 miles per hour in some other species—that this water is forced up, forming a mistlike spray.

Whales can eat underwater without getting water into their lungs, because a whale's windpipes lead directly from the blowhole or blowholes to the lungs. They do not connect with the mouth in any way. Strong muscles close the blowholes and keep them watertight.

Whales can't breathe automatically, the way land mammals do. They have to consciously open the blowholes to take in air. The way they breathe depends upon the length of time they stay submerged. Sperm whales inhale once for every minute spent underwater. After a thirty-minute dive they blow thirty times.

When preparing for a deep dive, a whale inhales rapidly several times. With each breath it replaces almost all of the air in its lungs—80 to 90 percent, according to some estimates. Humans and other land animals renew only about 10 to 15 percent of the air their lungs can hold.

Most whales usually stay underwater for only five to fifteen minutes. Fin whales and blue whales, however, sometimes stay under for forty minutes, and the champion divers, the sperm and bottlenose whales, can stay under for fifty to ninety minutes at a time. Sperm whales have been known to dive two miles below the surface. No one knows how deep bottlenose whales can go.

Although a humpback's lungs are as large as a Volkswagen car, a whale's lungs are no larger in proportion to its body size than a human's lungs are. Whales can hold their breath for much longer than humans can because their bodies are specially adapted to pressure. When a whale dives deeply, its lungs partially collapse. The air in the lungs is pushed into passages in the head and stored there until the whale returns to the surface. The heart slows; the body temperature drops; and blood leaves the tail, flippers, and skin and goes to the head and brain. As the whale rises, the stored air returns to the lungs and is exhaled explosively at the surface.

Deep-diving whales show their tail flukes when they dive or "sound." Flukes are a whale's trademark. Scientists can tell species apart by the shape and size of their flukes. They can identify individual humpback or gray whales by notches, bumps, or scars on the flukes, or the coloring of

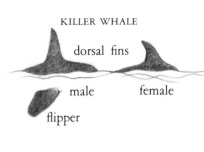

KILLER WHALE

dorsal fins

male female

flipper

the fluke blades. Like fingerprints, no two flukes are exactly alike. A shark had taken a bite from the fluke of the large gray whale that played with us in San Ignacio Lagoon. I will recognize her by that mark the next time I see her.

A whale's flukes grow horizontally (sideways), instead of vertically (up and down) like those of a fish. They have no bones, but tough fibers make them almost as strong as steel. Powerful muscles in the tail drive the great fan-shaped blades up and down and propel the whale through the water.

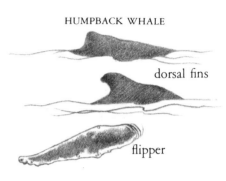

HUMPBACK WHALE

dorsal fins

flipper

It takes very little energy for whales to swim. Their bodies are better designed than any man-made missile or submarine. A fine oil lubricates their smooth, thin skin and reduces friction. Their extremely flexible and marvelously streamlined bodies glide through the water without a ripple. In addition, their bones are light and spongy, making them neutrally buoyant (they neither rise nor sink). These animals can stay at any given depth without effort.

Dorsal fins and flippers give whales stability and keep them right side up. The flippers rotate at the shoulders and are also used for steering and braking. Some whales have short flippers, but those of the gray whale may be fourteen feet long. The longest flippers belong to the humpback whale. They may be up to sixteen feet long.

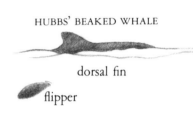

HUBBS' BEAKED WHALE

dorsal fin

flipper

Dorsal fins come in many sizes and shapes. That of a one-hundred-foot blue whale is only a foot high, while the fin of a thirty-foot killer whale is

SPERM WHALE

dorsal fin

flipper

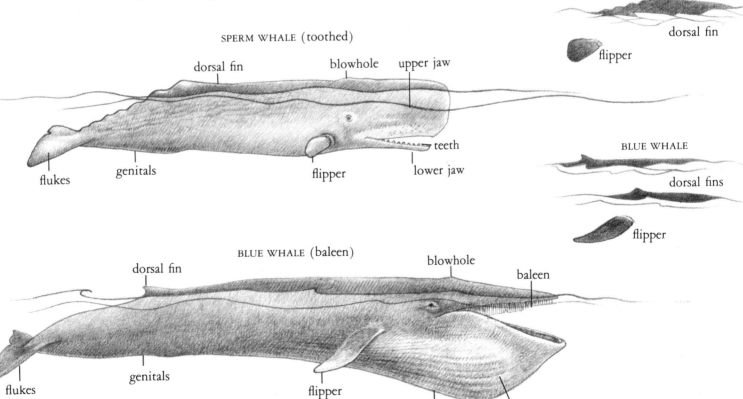

SPERM WHALE (toothed)

dorsal fin · blowhole · upper jaw

flukes · genitals · flipper · teeth · lower jaw

BLUE WHALE

dorsal fins

flipper

BLUE WHALE (baleen)

dorsal fin · blowhole · baleen

flukes · genitals · flipper · throat grooves · lower jaw

25

six feet tall. Some fins are triangular, and some are hooked like those of sharks. But whales are easy to tell from sharks because their flukes are horizontal instead of vertical. Not all whales have dorsal fins. Some—the right whale and bowhead—have smooth backs. Others, like the grays and sperms, have knobs and ridges down the middle of their backs.

The fastest of the toothed whales race along at twenty to thirty miles per hour. Most baleen whales cruise along at four miles per hour or less. But when they dive or want to put on a burst of speed, they are capable of tremendous power. The twelve-foot flukes of a forty-foot gray whale can drive the animal through the water at more than ten miles per hour. Sei (SAY) whales may reach speeds of thirty miles per hour, but they could not maintain this speed for long without overheating. Fortunately, it takes very little effort or speed for baleen whales to catch food.

gray whale feeding

insert: krill (2–3 in.)

26

Chapter 4

Sea Soup and Sonar

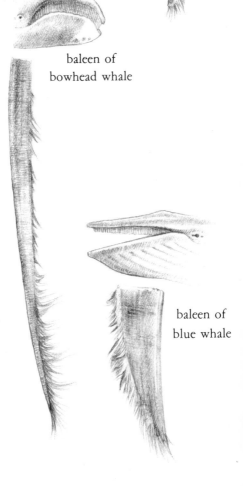

baleen of
humpback whale

baleen of
bowhead whale

baleen of
blue whale

A HUNGRY HUMPBACK WHALE DIVED BENEATH A SCHOOL OF TINY FISH and, while circling it, blew bubbles from its blowholes. The bubbles rose in a column, creating a net of bubbles around the fish. Then, with open mouth, the humpback surfaced inside the bubble net and feasted on the trapped fish.

Humpbacks, like all whales, are carnivores. They eat only animal food. Baleen whales eat small schooling fish and zooplankton such as krill and copepods (shrimplike sea animals two to six inches long). It takes a great amount of these tiny animals to feed such huge creatures—some whales eat eight thousand pounds every day. Fortunately, zooplankton is one of the most plentiful food sources in the ocean. During the summer krill, copepods, and schooling fish are so numerous in the Arctic and Antarctic oceans that the water looks like a thick, living soup.

Baleen whales spend their summers in the polar regions feasting on this sea soup. Those whales with very thick blubber eat only during the summer. They store up nutrition in their blubber and live off it in winter. Others seem to feed year-round.

The mouths of mysticetes are specially adapted for filtering or straining zooplankton and small fish from water. Between 150 and 700 baleen plates hang down, like the teeth of a comb, from a mysticete's upper jaw. These plates are from twelve inches to fifteen feet long. Baleen, which is sometimes called whalebone, is not bone but keratin, the same flexible material fingernails are made of. The inside edges of the plates are lined

baleen of gray whale

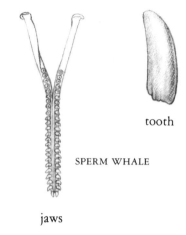

tooth

SPERM WHALE

jaws

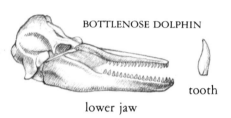

BOTTLENOSE DOLPHIN

tooth

lower jaw

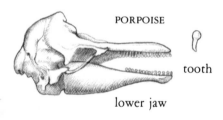

PORPOISE

tooth

lower jaw

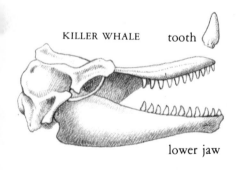

KILLER WHALE   tooth

lower jaw

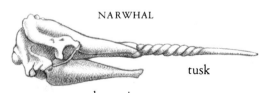

NARWHAL

tusk

lower jaw

with fine fringe, which acts as a sieve. Each species has a different kind of baleen, depending upon its feeding habits.

Right whales steam along the surface with their enormous cavelike jaws open, taking in huge amounts of water and zooplankton. The tiny sea animals are sifted out by the very long, narrow, finely fringed baleen while water spills through the sides of the whale's mouth or is pushed out by a tongue that may weigh as much as an adult elephant. The incredible heads of these whales are one-third as long as their sixty-foot bodies and may be as tall as a two-story building.

Rorquals, such as the humpbacks, fins, and blue whales, eat larger prey. They gulp their food instead of skimming it off the top of the water. They have shorter and wider baleen than that of the skimmers, and it has longer fringe. Their heads are much smaller, but their throats are pleated and expand like an accordion, enabling them to gulp or suck in great mouthfuls of sea soup. The pouches beneath a blue whale's jaws can hold up to four tons of sea soup. When full, the pouches contract, forcing the water out through the baleen, which traps the fish and zooplankton.

Fin whales sometimes swim around schools of small, fast-swimming fish, frightening them into tight groups to make bigger mouthfuls.

Gray whales have a different feeding method. They bulldoze furrows across the ocean floor with narrow, shovellike jaws, sucking in tiny bottom-dwelling crustaceans. As they surface, they push water and sediment through their short, coarse baleen with their three-thousand-pound tongues. Although you can't see gray whales feeding, you can tell where they have been. The water looks muddy, like a pond after a rain.

Most whales suck food into their mouths and swallow it whole into their three-chambered stomachs. Even the odontocetes don't chew their food, although a few crush it.

The number and kind of teeth a toothed whale has depend on the way the teeth are used. Odontoceti eat larger prey than baleen whales. Most have many sharp, cone-shaped teeth, which they use to hold the fast-swimming fish and slippery squid or octopus that are their favorite foods.

In some species, only males have visible teeth. Their teeth apparently are used only for fighting and are thicker and heavier than the holding teeth of other species.

Killer whales have forty-eight thick, heavy teeth. Their teeth are used

humpback whale (*M. novaeangliae*)
blowing bubbles around fish

29

BODY SHAPES
OF TOOTHED WHALES

SPERM WHALE (Physeteridae)

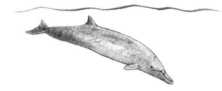

STEJNEGER'S BEAKED WHALE (Ziphiidae)

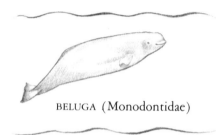

BELUGA (Monodontidae)

CHINESE RIVER DOLPHIN (Platanistidae)

DALL'S PORPOISE (Phocoenidae)

COMMON DOLPHIN (Delphinidae)

to tear chunks of flesh from seals, sea lions, dolphins, penguins, polar bears, and sometimes young whales. These fast, aggressive hunters often gather in packs to attack larger animals. They are the only whales known to eat warm-blooded animals, although false killer whales are suspected of doing so.

Most toothed whales have smaller, slenderer bodies than baleen whales because they must swim faster to catch their prey. Sperm whales normally swim ten miles per hour, while the more streamlined dolphins, whose flexible bodies change shape as they speed up, can swim up to twenty miles per hour. Some increase their speed and save energy by "porpoising"—alternately leaping free of the water and skimming along just below the surface, looking very much like skipping stones.

Like baleen whales, toothed whales are excellent hunters and employ other tactics as well as speed to capture fish.

Although some baleen whales may be able to follow odor trails, most whales have no sense of smell at all. Except for the killer whale, which can detect the only fish in a bucketful that has a pill in it and spit it out, their sense of taste is also weak. Most species can see quite well, both in and out of water, but muddy water limits vision to only a few feet, and in dark, deep water very few creatures can see anything. Therefore, sight is not very useful for toothed whales that eat below the surface. Whales have an extraordinarily good sense of hearing, however, and like bats they use sound to find their way around and to locate prey.

Underwater, hearing is a much more efficient way of getting information than vision. Sound travels through water four times as fast as it does in air, and it carries much farther and faster in water than light does. The opposite is true in air.

Some whales get information about their environment by making clicking sounds. These high-pitched, rapid-fire clicks bounce off objects such as underwater canyon walls and sea mountains. They are also used to locate food and to get more detailed information. This is called echolocation and is very much like the sonar used by navy ships, but it is much more sensitive.

Dolphins can make sounds that are up to ten times higher than human ears can hear. These high-pitched sounds do not travel as far as lower-pitched sounds, but with them a dolphin can locate a fish as small as one inch long and can tell the difference between two kinds of fish.

porpoising

Killer whale (*O. orca*) pursuing leopard seal

31

PORPOISE

triangular dorsal fin

rounded forehead

DOLPHIN

dorsal fin curves back toward tail

pronounced beak

The high-pitched sounds of toothed whales seem to be sent out through the melon—the fatty material in their foreheads. When these whales inspect something with sonar, they point their snouts toward the object and sweep it with sound waves by turning their heads from side to side. Divers report that when a dolphin points its beak at them, they not only hear the sounds but feel them vibrating in their skulls. Some scientists believe that toothed whales use the same kind of ultrasonic waves to stun their prey. Returning echoes may be picked up by the whale's ears and channeled through globs of fat in the lower jaw, but any part of the body can receive vibration.

Most baleen whales don't need detailed information to navigate, because they live in the open sea, but some may use sonar to find food.

With sound, whales inform themselves in detail about their place in their underwater world, other whales, unknown things, enemies, and food. They pass on this information to their fellow whales.

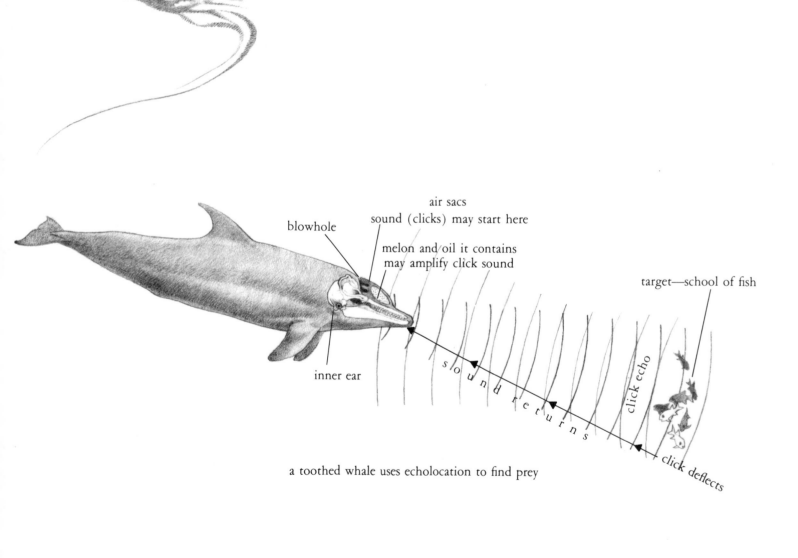

air sacs
sound (clicks) may start here

blowhole

melon and oil it contains
may amplify click sound

target—school of fish

inner ear

sound returns

click echo

click deflects

a toothed whale uses echolocation to find prey

Chapter 5
Whale Talk

FROM THE DECK OF ANOTHER SHIP IN THE WARM SEAS NEAR HAWAII, I LIS-tened to the song of a humpback whale. Every winter these waters are filled with songs sung by male humpbacks hanging motionless ten to a hundred feet below the surface. These weird, alien songs sound like those of birds, but are longer and louder. They may last thirty minutes and are repeated over and over, sometimes for several hours.

Why do these giants stand on their heads and sing hour after hour? What do their songs mean? Scientists think the songs have something to do with courting. Humpback whales go to warm waters in the Pacific and Atlantic oceans to mate and have babies. The songs may be dominance symbols like the antlers on a deer. The most skillful singer may win the most females.

All males in a single group sing the same song. But each year they add new parts, so it is quite different at the end of the season than it was at the beginning. The humpback is the only mammal, besides man, that com-poses its own songs.

While humpbacks are the only whales that sing, others chirp, whistle, and chatter at each other. Each whale has its own special "voice," just as humans do. The signal of one is unlikely to be mistaken for that of an-other.

Like most other mammals whales protest, threaten, and show distress with sounds—chirps, barks, squawks, grunts, and growls. A sharp, force-

humpback whale diving

ful crack seems to be an alarm call. They whistle to keep in touch and send information to one another with bursts of clicks. Dolphins can whistle and click at the same time.

Although humpbacks definitely make more sounds than any other whale, blue whales and sperm whales are the loudest. The blue whale's moaning and the sperm whale's clacking are the loudest sounds made by any animal alive today. They are louder than a jet engine or a shotgun blast.

It is speculated that before there were diesel-powered ships, power plants, and other human-made noises in the ocean, the low-pitched sounds of these baleen whales could be heard a thousand miles away. Today, with noise pollution, they can be heard for only a hundred miles.

Scientists are not certain how whales make sounds. Cetaceans don't have vocal cords, and the whistles are not made by the blowholes because the blowholes are closed when the sounds are made. Most scientists think that the clicks, grunts, moans, and whistles may be made by explosive movements of air from one air-filled cavity inside the head to another.

Whales have no outer ears. There are pin-sized openings just behind the eyes that lead to the inner ears, which are similar to those of humans. In some baleen whales the openings are plugged with wax so water can't get in, but this doesn't interfere with hearing. The ears of all whales are well adapted for underwater hearing. They are spaced far apart and are insulated from each other, so a whale hears different sounds with each ear. The bottlenose dolphin can pinpoint the exact spot where an object is located. Dolphins can hear higher-pitched sounds than any other animal. Baleen whales can hear an enemy a mile away.

Cetaceans have huge, complex brains. They need large brains to handle all of the information that they receive with their sensitive hearing systems. Some scientists think that whales use sounds to form mental pictures of objects and maps of their environment, the same way humans use sight. Toothed whales have larger brains than baleen whales. The sperm whale's twenty-pound brain is the largest brain on earth. Much of it is used for processing sounds.

No one knows how intelligent whales are. But many scientists think that dolphins are at least as intelligent as apes. Killer whales are thought to be the most intelligent of the dolphins. They learn twice as fast as other species. Many can learn a routine simply by observing it once.

Although a whale's eyes are relatively small, most cetaceans can see as well as a cat. They probably identify members of their species by coloring. Vision is also used to observe body movements of other whales, which, like most other animals, cetaceans use to send messages.

Dolphins open their mouths, arch their backs, or clap their jaws together to threaten one another. To show submission they turn their bodies sideways with mouths closed. Some whales slam their heads from side to side to threaten an intruder.

right whale
slapping flipper

Others lobtail. They stand on their heads in the water and swing their tails from side to side, making their massive flukes slap against the surface with a thundering noise as loud as a cannon. No one knows for certain why they do this. It may be some kind of signal, although calves sometimes appear to lobtail just for fun. There seems to be more lobtailing when strong winds whip up high waves and drown out vocal sounds. Sometimes lobtailing by one member will cause others to do the same until the whole herd is lobtailing at once! Dolphins slap their tails when they are angry or disturbed or when something has invaded their territory. Some whales slap their flippers as well as their flukes.

Many whales breach, or leap above the surface of the water. Swimming at top speed, the whale thrusts its flippers downward and shoots itself out of the water like a rocket. It then twists in midair and lands with a loud splash on its back or side. Humpbacks are the champion breachers, leaping completely clear of the water and landing on their backs. Usually whales breach three or four times in a row, but forty breaches made one after another by a single whale have been counted.

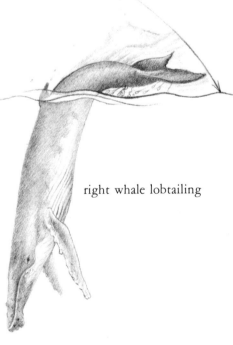

right whale lobtailing

right whale breaching

humpback whales lobtailing

common dolphins porpoising

Scientists don't know why whales breach, but some believe it is a way of saying, "Here I am!" to other whales. Others think it may be one way that males show off their strength. Some say these leapers are just getting rid of pests on their skin. Perhaps the whales want to see where they are so they can correct their course. Or they may breach just for the fun. Whatever the reason, it seems to be contagious. When one breaches, others often do too.

Whales also use touch to communicate. Hairs and whiskers along their chins and the tops of their heads may be touch organs that help them locate food (like the whiskers of a cat). But by far their most important touch organ is their very sensitive skin. They often stroke one another with their flippers and flukes and frequently rub their bodies together. Touching is especially important in courtship. It is said that when a human touches a dolphin, a bond of friendship is established.

Sounds hold herds of whales together and keep individuals in contact even though they may be far apart. When members are near, touching may keep order within the herd.

fin whales (B. *physalus*)

Chapter 6

World's Biggest Babies

ONCE TWO CETOLOGISTS WERE STUDYING WHALES IN SAN IGNACIO LAgoon when a baby gray whale pressed itself against the side of their inflatable skiff. The scientists were alarmed and tried to push it away. They knew that the baby's mother might think they would harm her offspring and might smash their boat. But the baby wouldn't budge. Before long they saw the hulking gray mass of the mother rising directly under them and her baby. To their great relief, she gently led the calf away from the boat.

All whales protect their young, but none as fiercely as a gray whale. Mother grays can be very dangerous if they think their babies are threatened. Whalers often called them devilfish because they sometimes smashed boats that came between them and their calves.

Newborn gray whales are fifteen feet long and weigh about fifteen hundred pounds. Big as they are, they are not the world's largest babies. That title belongs to the twenty-five-foot, eight-ton baby blue whales. A baby blue whale is longer than a school bus and heavier than a bull elephant!

Baby whales are called calves; their mothers, cows. Most cetaceans give birth to a single calf every year or two. Most newborns are large—at least one-third their mother's size—because they are born underwater and need the extra size and fat to prevent heat loss. They are well developed and look just like their mothers, but they may be a little darker in color.

Although a bit awkward at first, most calves can float as soon as they are born, and they go immediately to the surface to breathe. A calf that

gray whale and calf

adult gray whale pushes calf to the surface

can't surface by itself is pushed to the surface by its mother or another female whale who attends the birth. These attendants are sometimes called "aunties" but may actually be grandmothers.

Most calves are born tail first, so that the blowholes are the last to emerge. At birth the flukes are folded and the dorsal fin and flippers lie flat against the body. Like the wings of a butterfly, they are quite flexible for the first few hours, but then they stiffen rapidly. Sometimes a mother holds the baby at the surface until it can swim well.

During the first few weeks the calf is in constant body contact with its mother. It swims just behind her midsection. The water passing between their two bodies pulls it along so the baby barely needs to move its flukes to keep up.

A baby whale grows rapidly on its mother's rich milk. A blue whale calf may gain two hundred pounds every day, or ten pounds each hour! It doubles its weight in seven days, its length in three years.

The mother whale turns on her side to nurse her baby. The nipples, which are hidden in folds or slits on the mother's belly, drop down when nudged by the baby. The calf seizes the nipple between its tongue and the tip of its palate. Strong muscles around the mother's milk glands squirt huge quantities of milk into the baby's mouth. The calf nurses for only a few seconds at a time because it suckles underwater and can't hold its breath for long. Most continue to nurse for about a year, but some nurse for two years. And some are weaned in four months.

Mother whales continue to protect their young for several years after weaning. They are very affectionate and frequently stroke their calves. Sometimes they hold the calves on their bellies and pat them with their flippers.

A cow will not desert her calf in times of danger, even when protecting it puts her own life in jeopardy. She may shield her baby with her own body or push it out of danger with her snout. Some lift their babies on their flippers beyond an enemy's reach or catapult them away from danger with their flukes.

Like most baby animals, young whales are extremely curious. But their mothers will not allow them to stray far. If a bottlenose dolphin's calf ignores her whistle when she calls it back, the mother punishes her young one by nipping it gently, by holding it underwater for a few seconds, or by holding it above the water for a while.

bottlenose dolphin (*T. truncatus*) and calf

As the calves grow older, they begin to practice spyhopping, lobtailing, butting, bubbling, and breaching. Mostly they play—with seaweed, feathers, planks of wood, or just about anything, tossing and carrying these objects on their snouts. One of their favorite games is sliding off their mothers' backs or flukes. When a calf gets too rough, its mother may hold it in her armlike flippers until it settles down. Sometimes all the mothers and calves in a pod (family group) may join in a game of keep-away with a piece of kelp.

Calves mature at five to ten years old, but they still like to play. Many bow-ride—ride waves made by bows of ships—and surf on high waves during storms. Right whales hold their tails at right angles to the wind, letting the wind push them into shallow water, then circle back and go for another sail!

Usually, calves are three months or more old when they and their mothers join their herds for the annual trip to their feeding grounds. Every whale species has a route that it travels each season, probably using underwater landmarks or the earth's magnetic fields to keep to the same course year after year. The oceans are covered with networks of their migration trails.

Most baleen whales migrate to polar feeding grounds in the spring. They return to the warm waters of their favorite breeding areas the following fall. Some migrate great distances—up to thirteen thousand miles each year, the longest known migration of any mammal. Some toothed whales move only short distances, north and south or from inshore to offshore waters, with the seasons. Killer whales are the true nomads of the sea. They roam over great areas, traveling up to sixty-eight miles in a day.

Some scientists believe that cetaceans sleep little during their migrations. They may need only two or three hours' sleep a day, taken in short catnaps. Some seem to nap with only half of their brain at a time and with one eye open. Some appear to sleep just below the surface and must come up to breathe every few seconds. Others rest on the surface and appear to be sleeping rather soundly. Some even snore. When herds of whales doze, one or two stay awake and watch for danger.

Toothed whales tend to live and travel in large groups. Sometimes thousands of dolphins swim in single file, stretching thirty-five to forty miles across the sea.

Social groups of baleen whales generally seem to be smaller. Although

dolphins bow-riding

blue whale (*B. musculus*) calf and mother, playing

some mysticetes appear to be alone, it is possible that they actually are within hearing distance of many other whales that are scattered far apart. Some are known to live and travel in harem bands of fifty to a hundred individuals led by old males. Scientists believe that the younger males in these pods defend the calves and females in times of danger. Others live in pods led by females. These are usually groups of related mothers and young.

There seems to be a strong support system among some Odontoceti. It is believed that members of at least some species come to one another's aid in times of trouble. Members of a pod have been observed gathering around a wounded or ill individual. They appear to hold it on the surface so that it can breathe, until it can swim again.

This social bond may explain why, among some species, if the leader becomes stranded on the beach, the whole school will strand alongside it. Nothing, except the leader's death, can induce them to leave.

Courtship among all whales is usually accompanied by much caressing, gentle nipping, and racing around at full speed. Some males mate with only one female, others mate with any available female, while still others live in harems, one male with several females. Males in harem schools compete for females as do mountain goats or deer. The backs of male beaked, sperm, and humpback whales bear many scars from their fights.

In some species only half the females bear young in any one year. The other half help care for and protect the young of the school. They "baby-sit" while mothers eat. Most calves are born about a year after mating.

No one knows for sure how long whales might live if they were not caught or did not die of disease, though estimates exist. The approximate age of a dead baleen whale can be determined. Its earplugs have dark and light rings similar to the rings on a tree trunk. Scientists know how many of these rings are deposited each year and can estimate the age of the whale by counting them. The teeth of toothed whales have similar rings, but it is not certain how many layers are deposited each year, so this method is less reliable. Scientists believe that baleen whales might live up to eighty years.

Scientists have learned many things about these creatures that live in families, play in storms, talk to one another, and care for one another in times of trouble. But there is still much more to learn.

a weak dolphin is supported at the surface

Chapter 7

Friends or Foes?

CETOLOGISTS SPEND THEIR LIVES STUDYING WHALES. IT IS AN OCCUPATION that is full of surprises.

While studying humpbacks near the coast of South America, a scientist attempted to get a closer look at a large animal twenty feet below him. When he tried to descend, however, the whale flipped its great flukes, and a surge of water popped him to the surface like a cork. Three times this happened. Finally the diver felt a faint suction, and the playful whale helped him descend.

Even though humans were once whales' worst enemies, whales do not hurt divers. In fact, these friendly creatures seem to take great care to avoid striking divers with a fluke or a flipper. In return, cetologists try to study whales without hurting or disturbing them. Many times the whales seem to be as curious about the scientists as the scientists are about the whales.

Curious dolphins are sometimes attracted to ships by music. So a group studying wild spotted dolphins in the Caribbean played music to keep them close enough to observe.

To the scientists' surprise, it seemed to them that the dolphins were mimicking sounds coming from the boat.

Later, one dolphin watched as a scientist dropped, feet first, to the bottom. It followed him, dropping tail first. The diver lay on the sea floor to adjust his equipment; the dolphin lay on the sea floor, too. Then the scientist stood on the bottom, and the dolphin stood on its tail on the bottom. The scientist thought that this dolphin was mimicking his actions as well as the sounds! Other scientists are not convinced that this was what was happening.

Captive dolphins are eager to cooperate in experiments and seem to do them more for approval than for reward. They sometimes learn routines by watching another perform. Perhaps it is possible that a wild dolphin could do the same.

Scientists are looking for ways to test the intelligence of these incredible creatures. Researchers are trying to discover what whales are saying when they talk to one another. Some cetologists are attempting to decipher whale conversations. Others are using symbol and sign languages, similar to those used with chimpanzees, to teach dolphins human language. They hope that someday a human may be able to talk to a cetacean. Think of all the wonderful things dolphins could tell us if they succeed!

Other scientists are trying to learn where whales travel. They implant radio-equipped tags in the whales' thick blubber, then monitor them by satellite.

Immunologists are looking at antibodies found in whale blood. These antibodies may help in leukemia and cancer research. Killer whales may be the only mammals that can regrow lost flesh without forming scar tissue. Scientists are trying to learn how they do this.

Many scientists are trying to solve the puzzle of why entire schools of toothed whales swim ashore and become stranded. An ill or wounded baleen whale goes ashore to keep from drowning, but when entire herds of odontocetes strand, they aren't all ill. It appears that in some species, the leader may be. Perhaps, in these cases, the rest of the herd strand because they will not desert their leader. But this does not seem to explain all strandings.

Scientists have noted that most mass strandings occur in areas where the sandy bottom slopes gradually. In such places it is difficult to get good sonar echoes. Since odontocetes rely on echo-location, this may be a possible cause of some strandings.

More recent studies suggest still another possible reason. There is some evidence that whales have magnetic sensing organs similar to those of birds, bees, and sharks. The studies suggest that cetaceans use extra-strong

stranded pilot whales

bridled spotted dolphins (*S. attenuata*)

lamprey
(up to 33 in.)

whale lice
(up to 1 in.)

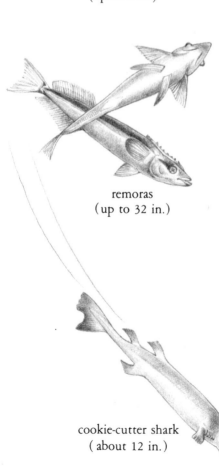

remoras
(up to 32 in.)

cookie-cutter shark
(about 12 in.)

magnetic fields, such as those around undersea volcanoes, to mark the boundaries of feeding and resting areas. Sharks and migrating birds use their sensors to stay on course when migrating. Areas of magnetic fields stretch around the earth from the North Pole to the South Pole. Perhaps whales also use their magnetic sensors to detect and follow ocean highways marked by the north-south troughs lying along the ocean floor. The beaches where most whales become stranded have low magnetic fields. Perhaps the cetaceans get lost and make a wrong turn where the magnetism is weak, then accidentally become stranded.

Others suggest that whales may sometimes accidentally become beached when pursuing food or fleeing from predators. Some whales may become disoriented when, as sometimes happens, their ears are infested by parasites.

Although ear parasite infestation can be a serious problem for whales, scientists have learned that this is not the only parasite or pest that plagues cetaceans. Many kinds of creatures prey on them.

Lamprey eels suck their blood. Small cookie-cutter sharks cut little round plugs from their sides and bellies. Large sharks take bites from their flukes, flippers, or fins. Barnacles attach themselves to a baby whale's skin soon after it is born and may remain there for life. Some whales carry half a ton of barnacles embedded in their hides. Tiny crablike creatures called whale lice cling with sharp claws to the skin of many whales.

However, not all creatures accompanying whales are pests. Some help the whales. Small fish and remoras, or sucker fish, eat whale lice, and sometimes seagulls land on a whale's back or head and feed on the pests.

Although a polar bear might occasionally kill a narwhal or beluga, sharks and killer whales are a whale's main predators. A whale's only defense against these enemies is to flee to shallow water or strike back with its huge head or flukes, either of which can deal a deadly blow.

Once humans killed whales by the thousands every year for meat, whalebone, and oil. Five species—the blue, right, bowhead, humpback, and gray—were near extinction. Then in 1972 the U.S. Marine Mammal Protection Act stopped the widespread slaughter of whales by Americans. No United States citizen may catch or kill any marine mammal anywhere in the world without special permission from the Marine Mammal Commission. Most other nations have similar laws.

Objects once made of whalebone are now made of plastic. Scientists

polar bear with narwhal (*M. monoceros*)

49

have found that oil from the jojoba bean is actually better than whale oil for most uses. It is hoped that whale oil used to make margarine, medicines, and cosmetics will be replaced by jojoba bean oil. Jojoba bushes are being grown experimentally on large plantations in the southwestern part of the United States.

Some whales are still taken for food, and some are killed accidentally in fish nets. Fishermen shoot many dolphins in the Pacific because the dolphins rob their hooks, and they have been unable to find any other way to keep these clever animals from taking their fish.

It is important that we find solutions to these problems. Much progress has already been made. The gray whale has returned from near extinction three times. The humpback is recovering, and the number of dolphins killed by yellowfin tuna fishermen has dropped from four hundred thousand in 1972 to fewer than twenty thousand in 1984. That is a good beginning.

We have much more to gain from being friends to whales than from being foes. Whales are renewable resources if properly managed. They are far more valuable than the food, oil, or baleen for which they are hunted; other materials can take the place of these. We can never replace a magnificent whale once it is gone.

These friendly travelers are an important part of the ecology of our planet. They have occupied a far greater portion of it, and for a much longer period of time, than humans. They have been remarkably successful in adapting to their environment and have met its challenges without destroying it. Can we do the same?

A Glossary of Whales

Chapter 8

A Glossary of Whales

AMAZON RIVER DOLPHIN *(Inia geoffrensis)*—Also called boutu by river people who consider it sacred. An odontocete of the Platanistidae family. This seven-foot, 132-pound river dolphin is found only in shallow, muddy waters of the Amazon and Orinoco river systems of South America. It has 96 to 136 teeth. Those at the front of its long, narrow beak are conical; the molarlike teeth in the back are used to crush fish and mollusks. The Amazon River dolphin has broad flippers, a broad dorsal hump instead of a fin, and wide, notched flukes. Adults are pale gray to almost white. The thirty-inch newborns are dark gray. This rare dolphin has tiny eyes but good vision, and large ear holes with excellent hearing.

Amazon River dolphin (*Inia geoffrensis*) 7 ft.

ANDREW'S BEAKED WHALE *(Mesoplodon bowdoini)*—Also called

deep-crested whale and splaytooth beaked whale. An odontocete of the Ziphiidae family. This thirteen-foot, 1.2-ton beaked whale is quite similar to Hubbs' beaked whale and may be the same species. It is known only from six stranded specimens in temperate areas of the Indian and Pacific oceans. Males have a pair of massive, protruding six-inch teeth in the middle of the lower jaw. The back and sides of males are covered with many scars, presumably from fights with other males. The back is gray, grading to light gray on the belly. The flukes are unnotched.

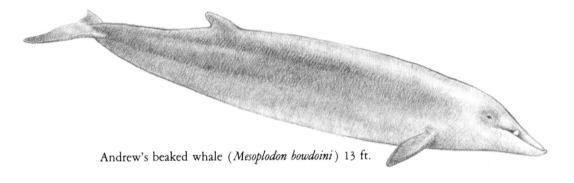

Andrew's beaked whale *(Mesoplodon bowdoini)* 13 ft.

ANTILLEAN BEAKED WHALE—*See* GULF STREAM BEAKED WHALE.

ARCHAEOCETI (Ancient Whales)—An order of whales, known only from

fossils, that were extinct by the middle of the Miocene epoch. These whales had incisors, canines, and grinding teeth. In most, the nostrils were located only a short distance from the tip of the jaw. There were four families in this group of whales. The most primitive, the Protocetidae, were seven to thirty feet long and had small limbs and snouts shaped like those of reptiles. The Dorudontidae were twenty feet long and had a typical whale shape. Basilosauridae were eel-like or snakelike. Patriocetidae were the most modern of the ancient whales. Their nostrils were placed far back on the snout.

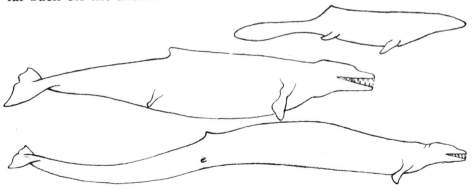

ARCH BEAKED WHALE—*See* HUBBS' BEAKED WHALE.

ARCTIC WHALE—*See* BOWHEAD WHALE.

ARNOUX'S BEAKED WHALE *(Berardius arnuxii)*—Also called southern fourtoothed whale. An odontocete of the Ziphiidae family. This thirty-two-foot, seven-ton whale is the second largest beaked whale. It is quite similar to Baird's beaked whale and may be the same species. The forehead is bulbous and the snout is like a dolphin's. Both sexes have two pairs of wide, triangular teeth at the tip of the lower jaw, which extends beyond the upper, exposing the teeth. This whale has a small fin; long, broad, rounded flippers; and large, slightly notched flukes. It is dark blue-gray with darker flukes, flippers, and back. Newborn calves are twelve feet long. Arnoux's beaked whale has never been seen alive. It is known from fifty stranded specimens found in the southern hemisphere. It eats squid and mollusks.

Arnoux's beaked whale (*Berardius arnuxii*) 32 ft.

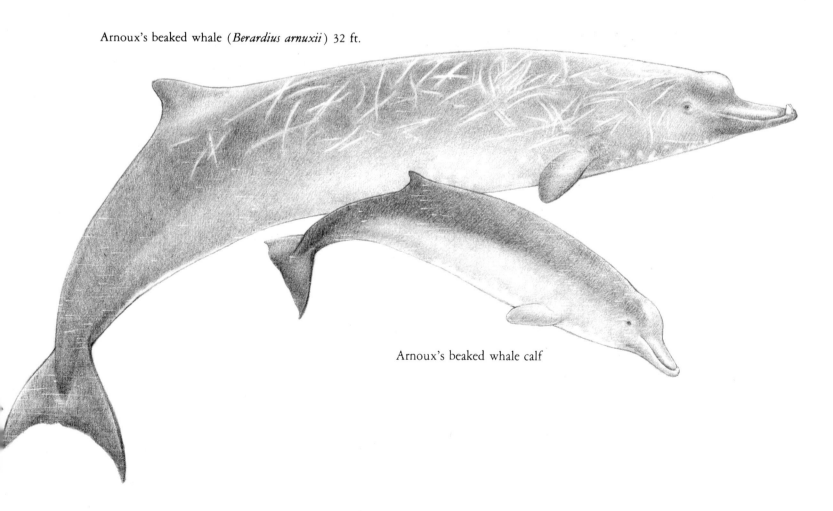

Arnoux's beaked whale calf

ATLANTIC HUMP-BACKED DOLPHIN *(Sousa teuszii)*—Also

called West African humpback dolphin. An odontocete of the Delphinidae family. Little is known about this seven-foot, 270-pound oceanic dolphin. Its head resembles that of the bottlenose dolphin, but the beak is longer. The small dorsal fin is located on a long, low ridge at midback. The flukes are deeply notched. Calves are creamy white, darkening to pale slate gray on the back as they grow older. This fish-eater lives in tropical coastal waters off West Africa, occasionally entering rivers. It is believed to be closely related to the Indo-Pacific hump-backed dolphin.

Atlantic hump-backed dolphin (*Sousa teuszii*) 7 ft.

ATLANTIC SPOTTED DOLPHIN *(Stenella plagiodon)*—Also called

spotter dolphin. An odontocete of the Delphinidae family. This seven-foot, 242-pound oceanic dolphin is similar to the bridled spotted dolphin but is more robust, and its tall dorsal fin is more sharply hooked. The slender head has a long, narrow beak. The flippers and flukes are like those of bottlenose dolphins. This dolphin's back is dark gray, covered with light spots. The sides and belly are lighter gray to white with darker spots. Herds of several thousand live offshore in warm temperate and tropical waters of the Atlantic, moving inshore to calve. Atlantic spotted dolphins seem to have home ranges two hundred to three hundred nautical miles in diameter. They eat fish and squid.

Atlantic spotted dolphin (*Stenella plagiodon*) 7 ft.

ATLANTIC WHITE-SIDED DOLPHIN (*Lagenorhynchus acutus*)

—An odontocete of the Delphinidae family. This nine-foot, 420-pound, thick-bodied oceanic dolphin eats fish and squid. It has a sloping forehead; 160 sharp, pointed teeth; a tall, hooked, sharply pointed dorsal fin; and shallowly notched flukes. The back is black. The white of the belly extends rather high up the sides, well above the sickle-shaped flippers. A gray streak separates the white and black. Behind and below the fin is a yellow or tan patch. The short, thick snout is black and gray. This dolphin lives offshore in the North Atlantic. In summer small groups go inshore to calve. Calves are 3.5 feet long at birth and weigh seventy-five pounds.

Atlantic white-sided dolphins (*Lagenorhynchus acutus*) 9 ft.

BAIRD'S BEAKED WHALE *(Berardius bairdii)*—Also known as giant
bottlenose whale and northern fourtooth whale. An odontocete of the
Ziphiidae family. This forty-foot, ten-ton whale is the largest beaked
whale. Females are larger than males. It is quite similar to Arnoux's
beaked whale and is possibly a northern version of that species. Only its
size and gestation period are different. The seventeen-month gestation period of this whale is longer than that of any other mammal except the
elephant. Newborns are fifteen feet long. This whale has a small head
with a steep, bulbous melon and a snout like a dolphin's. Both sexes have
two pairs of teeth at the tip of the lower jaw, which extends four inches
beyond the upper. The body, dorsal fin, and flippers are typical of beaked
whales. The flukes are unnotched. This fast deep-diver is dark bluish gray
above, with a lighter belly and patches of white on the throat. It lives far
offshore in the North Pacific in small groups, each led by a male. Rivalry
among males for harems results in many scars. Baird's beaked whale eats
squid, octopus, lobster, and starfish.

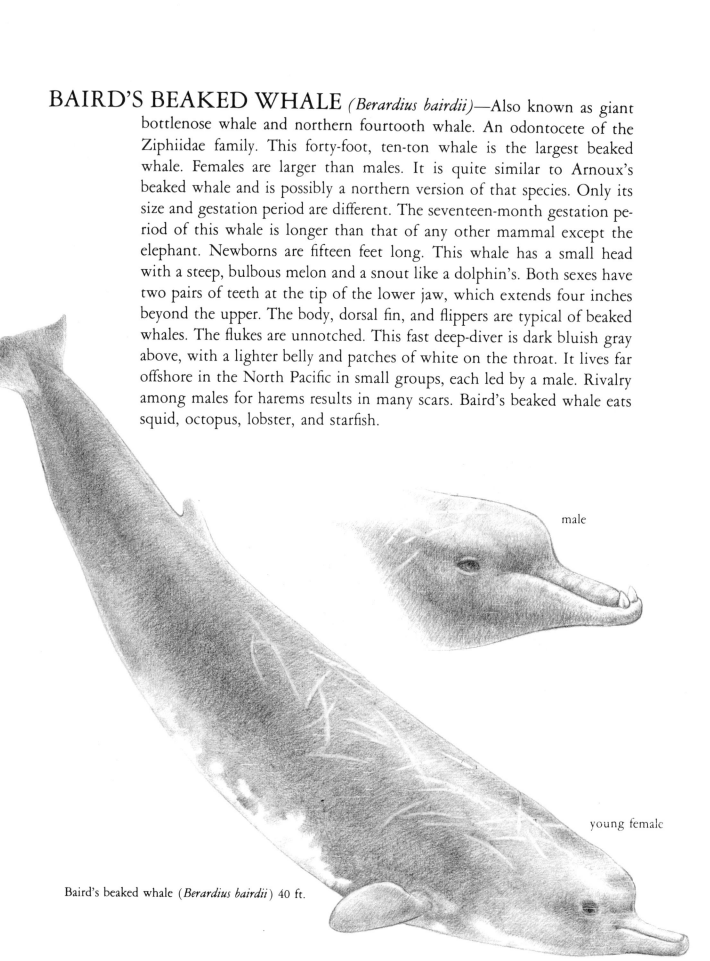

male

young female

Baird's beaked whale (*Berardius bairdii*) 40 ft.

BALAENIDAE (Right Whales)—A family of baleen whales that have very large heads (up to one-third of their body length) and very long, narrow baleen—up to fifteen feet in some species. The long upper jaw is thin and arched. These skim-feeders eat the smallest zooplankton. They have no throat pleats, and except for the pygmy right whale, which has a small one, they have no dorsal fins. Like all Mysticeti, they have two blowholes. There are three species in this family: the bowhead, right whale, and pygmy right whale. These whales range in size from sixteen to sixty-five feet. Females are usually larger than males. They are found worldwide in temperate and polar waters. They are called right whales because they are slow, have a lot of blubber, and float when dead, which made them easy to catch and therefore the "right whales" to hunt.

BALAENOPTERIDAE (Rorqual Whales)—A family of baleen whales that have small dorsal fins and large flippers. Most have long, slender snouts with moderately short baleen. The throat has many pleats or grooves and expands like an accordion as the whale swims along the surface gulping great mouthfuls of krill, zooplankton, small schooling fish, and water. The six species in this family include the blue whale, Bryde's whale, fin whale, humpback whale, minke whale, and sei whale. The blue whale is the largest animal that has ever lived. Rorquals range in size from twenty-eight to one hundred feet. Females are usually larger than males. They are found worldwide.

BALEEN WHALES—*See* MYSTICETI.

BEAKED WHALES—A family of toothed whales. *See* ZIPHIIDAE.

BEIJI—*See* CHINESE RIVER DOLPHIN.

BELUGA *(Delphinapterus leucas)*—Also called belukha, sea canary, and white whale. An odontocete of the Monodontidae family. This eighteen-foot, one-ton toothed whale has a long, robust body with no dorsal fin; a small head with a soft, bulbous melon, a short, broad beak, and up to forty teeth; short, broad, paddlelike flippers; and broad, notched flukes. It eats fish, squid, and bottom-dwelling crustaceans. The thick, completely white skin of an adult camouflages it in the icy Arctic. The four-foot newborns are dark gray. These sociable whales live in groups of thousands in shallow bays, river mouths, and deep waters of all Arctic seas. Belugas were once hunted commercially. Whalers called them sea canaries because of the variety of sounds they make. They are still heavily hunted by natives. They are quite playful when kept in captivity.

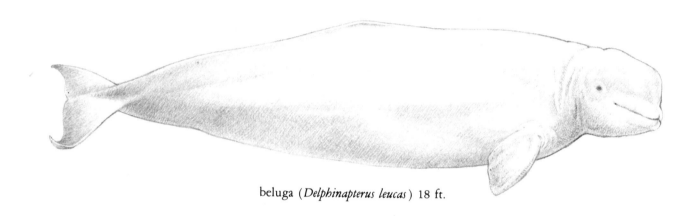

beluga (*Delphinapterus leucas*) 18 ft.

BELUKHA—*See* BELUGA.

BENGUELA DOLPHIN—*See* HEAVISIDE'S DOLPHIN.

BERING SEA BEAKED WHALE—*See* STEJNEGER'S BEAKED WHALE.

BLACK DOLPHIN (*Cephalorhynchus eutropia*)—Also called Chilean dolphin. An odontocete of the Delphinidae family. Little is known about this shy five-foot, 120-pound oceanic dolphin. Its broad, flat forehead merges into the beak. It has sixty round-tipped teeth, a small, rounded dorsal fin and flippers, and notched flukes. This dolphin has a dark cape with gray patches down the sides, a white throat and belly, a small white patch behind the flippers, and a very thin white line around the lips. It lives in cold shallow coastal waters off Chile in groups of eight to fourteen. It eats squid and shrimp.

black dolphin (*Cephalorhynchus eutropia*) 5 ft.

BLACK PORPOISE—*See* BURMEISTER'S PORPOISE.

BLACKCHIN DOLPHIN—*See* PEALE'S DOLPHIN.

BLACKFISH—*See* KILLER WHALE.

BLAINVILLE'S BEAKED WHALE (*Mesoplodon densirotris*)—Also called dense-beaked whale. An odontocete of the Ziphiidae family. This sixteen-foot, one-ton beaked whale is little known. Males have a pair of huge eight-inch teeth, set eight inches from the tip of the lower jaw. These teeth protrude like a pair of horns. Blainville's beaked whale has short flippers and a large, hooked dorsal fin. The unnotched flukes sometimes bulge outward at the center. The back is black or dark gray; the belly is lighter. The blow shoots forward at a sharp angle. This whale lives in small groups in tropical and warm temperate waters of all oceans. It eats squid.

Blainville's beaked whale (*Mesoplodon densirostris*) 16 ft.

BLUE WHALE *(Balaenoptera musculus)*—Also called sulphur bottom whale. A mysticete of the Balaenopteridae family. This rorqual whale is the largest animal known. It averages about ninety feet, but some females are more than one hundred feet long and weigh up to 180 tons. A newborn calf is twenty-four feet long and weighs about 2 tons. The blue whale has a streamlined head, a broad snout with a ridge down the center, a four-bristled minimustache, and a sparse beard of forty long hairs. Sixty to ninety long throat pleats accommodate enormous mouthfuls of food. Up to eight hundred plates of forty-inch-long black baleen line the upper jaw. This whale has small flippers; a tiny dorsal fin set far back near the twenty-foot-wide, slightly notched triangular flukes; and a thirty-foot, cone-shaped spout. Its color is a mottled blue-gray. The flipper tips and underside are much lighter than the back. This whale lives in close-knit family groups of three or four in deep water of all oceans of the world, but

blue whale (*Balaenoptera musculus*) 90–100 ft.

blue whale calf

it is most often seen in the southern hemisphere. In summer blue whales feed in polar waters on zooplankton—up to four tons a day. They migrate to equatorial waters to breed and calve. They travel about six to eight miles per hour but are capable of going thirty miles per hour. They are now rare, but some populations are increasing.

The somewhat smaller pygmy blue whale, a subspecies of the blue whale, lives in the southern hemisphere. Its maximum length is seventy-two feet. *See* PYGMY BLUE WHALE.

BOTTLENOSE DOLPHIN *(Tursiops truncatus)*—An odontocete of the

Delphinidae family. This gracefully streamlined 440-pound oceanic dolphin is the best known of all whales. It can be up to fourteen feet long. It is greatly attracted to humans and is the dolphin most often seen in marine parks and aquariums. Up to one hundred fairly large conical teeth line the mouth, which has an upward curve that gives this dolphin a permanent grin. It has a bulbous melon that rises steeply from the short, stubby beak. Its tall, hooked dorsal fin sits at midback, and its broad-based flippers taper to a curved tip. The curved flukes are deeply notched. The bottlenose dolphin is usually dark gray on the back, with lighter sides shading to a white belly. Newborns are 3.5 feet long and weigh seventy pounds. This dolphin lives in distinct herds that are found worldwide except in polar regions. It moves toward the equator in the autumn. This species lives both inshore and offshore, but most often inshore. It hunts cooperatively and eats a wide variety of fish and invertebrates. It can dive to two thousand feet.

bottlenose dolphin (*Tursiops truncatus*) 14 ft.

BOUTU—*See* AMAZON RIVER DOLPHIN.

BOWHEAD WHALE *(Balaena mysticetus)*—Also called Arctic whale and Greenland right whale. A mysticete of the Balaenidae family. This fifty-five-foot, 110-ton right whale has the longest baleen of any whale and the largest head of any animal in the world. Its enormous triangular head is one-third of its body length. The roof of its mouth is as high as a two-story building, and its tongue weighs a ton. Its dark gray baleen measures up to fifteen feet long. Over seven hundred plates hang from its huge upper jaw. This baleen whale has no throat pleats or dorsal fin. Its flippers are six feet long. The broad, deeply notched flukes are twenty-five feet across and have pointed tips. The two blowholes are widely separated,

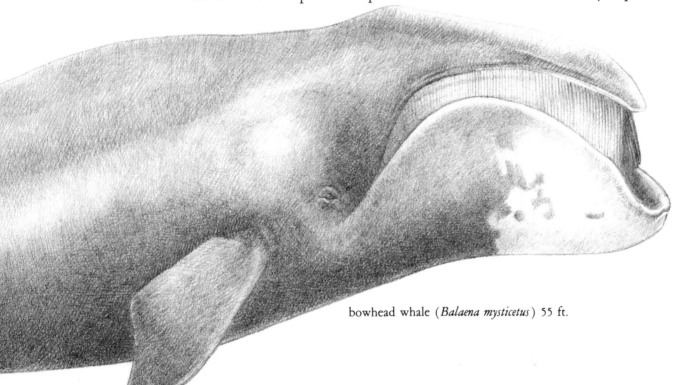

bowhead whale *(Balaena mysticetus)* 55 ft.

and the twenty-three-foot spout is V-shaped. Bowheads are usually completely black except for a white patch on the chin that is decorated with a row of dark spots, and a gray spot near the flukes. They generally travel alone or in groups of up to six. The bowhead lives farther north than any other whale, mostly in shallow coastal waters near the ice's edge in the Arctic Ocean. It migrates to the Bering Sea to breed and calve. Newborns are probably ten to fourteen feet long. This skim-feeder eats copepods and krill. Its blubber is up to two feet thick. Bowheads may be the rarest large animals in the world. Fewer than three thousand exist. Although they are now protected, some are still hunted by Alaskan Eskimos.

BRIDLED SPOTTED DOLPHIN *(Stenella attenuata)*—Also called

Pacific spotted dolphin and spotted dolphin. An odontocete of the Delphinidae family. This eight-foot, 220-pound oceanic dolphin is thirty-six to thirty-nine inches long when born. Most are dark gray, fading to lighter gray on the sides and belly, with light-colored spots in the dark areas and dark spots in the light areas. This dolphin has a very distinct beak; large, pointed flippers; and a tall, hooked fin. It lives worldwide in tropical waters near coastal areas and in deep offshore water. This surface-feeder has up to 160 tiny pointed teeth and eats squid, fish, and shrimp. One of the fastest whales, it can swim up to twenty miles per hour. It bow-rides and leaps high into the air. Schools of tuna associate with herds of these dolphins. Sometimes the dolphins are trapped in the purse seines (large nets) of tuna fishermen.

bridled spotted dolphin calf

bridled spotted dolphins *(Stenella attenuata)* 8 ft.

BRYDE'S WHALE *(Balaenoptera edeni)*—Also called tropical whale. A mysticete of the Balaenopteridae family. This forty-five-foot, thirteen-ton rorqual whale has a broad, flat head with a long, slender, pointed snout. Three prominent ridges extend from the two blowholes to the snout. Bryde's whale has 740 slate-gray, eighteen-inch baleen plates hanging from its upper jaws, and forty to fifty long throat pleats. The small, hooked dorsal fin has a ragged edge. The flippers are slender and pointed. The spout shoots up thirteen feet. Newborns are thirteen feet long. This dark gray whale closely resembles the sei and fin whales in shape and form. It lives in small groups or singly in tropical and subtropical waters around the world, often near the shore—especially during breeding and calving season—but may migrate to offshore waters with food sources. This whale eats schooling fish and zooplankton and feeds year-round. It is the only rorqual that dosen't feed in polar regions.

Bryde's whale (*Balaenoptera edeni*) 45 ft.

BURMEISTER'S PORPOISE *(Phocoena spinipinnis)*—Also called black porpoise. An odontocete of the Phocoenidae family. This six-foot, 110-pound porpoise is rarely seen alive. About a dozen have been caught in fishermen's nets. It has the same body shape as the common dolphin, but its head is a little smaller, has no beak, and has a less rounded forehead. It has seventy spade-shaped teeth. Its triangular dorsal fin is quite different from that of any other whale. It is located nearer the tail, leans rearward, and has three rows of sharp spines on the front edge. The large, broad flippers taper to a blunt point. This porpoise is deep gray to black, shading to a pale belly and chin. Newborns are probably about eighteen inches long. Burmeister's porpoise lives in shallow coastal waters off South America around the Strait of Magellan. It eats squid and fish.

Burmeister's porpoise (*Phocoena spinipinnis*) 6 ft.

CAA'ING WHALE—*See* LONG-FINNED PILOT WHALE.

CHILEAN DOLPHIN—*See* BLACK DOLPHIN.

CHINESE RIVER DOLPHIN *(Lipotes vexillifer)*—Also called beiji and Yangtze River dolphin. An odontocete of the Platanistidae family. This 7.5-foot, 170-pound river dolphin lives only in the Yangtze (Changjiang) River system and some connecting lakes. Its steep forehead drops to a long, narrow beak with a slightly upturned tip, like that of a duck. It has fairly long flukes, up to 140 small teeth, and broad, rounded flippers. Its triangular dorsal fin sits behind midback. It has very small eyes that are placed high on the head. Its back and sides are generally pale smoky gray, and the belly is grayish white. Newborns are about thirty inches long. This slow swimmer dredges fish, eel, and shrimp from the muddy river bottom.

Chinese river dolphin (*Lipotes vexillifer*) 7.5 ft.

CLYMENE DOLPHIN *(Stenella clymene)*—Also called helmet dolphin and short-snouted spinner dolphin. An odontocete of the Delphinidae family. This six-foot, 165-pound oceanic dolphin is little known and probably rare. It is similar to the spinner dolphin, but it has fewer teeth (a total of two hundred), a much shorter beak, and a different color pattern. It is medium to dark gray on the back and sides, with a white belly, light and dark stripes on the sides, and a distinctive line running from the blowhole to the tip of the beak. It has a tall, hooked dorsal fin and notched flukes. It lives in the open seas and deep coastal tropical and subtropical waters of the Atlantic. Clymene dolphins eat squid and small fish.

Clymene dolphin (*Stenella clymene*) 6 ft.

COCHITO—*See* GULF PORPOISE.

COMMERSON'S DOLPHIN *(Cephalorhynchus commersonii)*—Also called piebald dolphin. An odontocete of the Delphinidae family. This five-foot, 110-pound oceanic dolphin has a thick, stocky body. Unlike most other members of the genus, it somewhat resembles a porpoise with its sloping forehead and no beak. But its 120 small teeth are conical. It has a rounded dorsal fin slightly behind midback; small, rounded flippers; and broad, notched flukes. From the head to the flippers, and from the dorsal fin to the flukes, it is black. The rest of the body is white. This dolphin lives in shallow coastal waters of the southern hemisphere. It eats krill, squid, crab, small fish, and shrimp, frequently feeding on or near the bottom.

Commerson's dolphin (*Cephalorhynchus commersonii*) 5 ft.

COMMON DOLPHIN *(Delphinus delphis)*—An odontocete of the Delphinidae family. This seven-foot, 180-pound oceanic dolphin is the most commonly seen dolphin. It has a six- to ten-inch beak and a tall, hooked dorsal fin set at midback. The broad, deeply notched flippers taper to a point. The common dolphin is distinctively colored. The pattern is quite variable, and males are patterned differently from females. The beak, back, flippers, fin, and flukes are usually black. The chest and belly are white or cream. The sides have a crisscross pattern, with gray on the back flank and a patch of tan on the forward flank. Newborns are thirty-six inches long. Herds of many hundreds or thousands live offshore in all tropical and temperate waters of the world. A short-snouted form lives in inshore waters of tropical seas near the Indian Ocean and the Sea of Cortez. The common dolphin is not known to migrate, although it does travel a lot. It eats fish and squid and can dive to 920 feet.

common dolphin (*Delphinus delphis*) 6 ft.

COMMON PORPOISE—*See* HARBOR PORPOISE.

COMMON RORQUAL—*See* FIN WHALE.

CUVIER'S BEAKED WHALE *(Ziphius cavirostris)*—Also called goose beaked whale. An odontocete of the Ziphiidae family. This twenty-foot, 3.5-ton whale is one of the best-known beaked whales and one of the most widely distributed cetaceans. It lives everywhere but in polar waters. It is rarely seen, however, because it lives in deep water and is usually shy of ships. It has a long, robust body and a relatively small head with a distinct neck, a sloping forehead, and a short, stubby beak. The lower jaw extends beyond the upper, exposing two three-inch conical teeth at its tip. The small, rounded flippers fold into flipper pockets (depressions on the sides). The hooked, fifteen-inch dorsal fin sits far behind the midpoint of the whale's back. The flukes have almost no notch. The back is dark rust brown, slate gray, or fawn. The belly, and often the head, is paler. The low, inconspicuous spout projects slightly forward and to the left. Newborns are seven feet long. This whale eats squid, crab, and deep-water fish. It can stay submerged for twenty-five minutes.

Cuvier's beaked whale (*Ziphius cavirostris*) 20 ft.

DALL'S PORPOISE *(Phocoenoides dalli)*—Also called spray porpoise. An odontocete of the Phocoenidae family. Except for its teeth, this six-foot, 270-pound porpoise is unlike other members of its family. It is extremely stocky and powerfully built. It has a small, flattened, beakless head; small, pointed flippers; and broad flukes. The small, triangular dorsal fin is a little forward of center. Up to one hundred small, spade-shaped teeth line the small mouth. The body is black with a large white patch on the sides and belly and with white tips on the flukes, flippers, and fin. A few are nearly all white. These are sometimes called True's porpoises. Newborns are 3.5 feet long. Dall's porpoise is the fastest cetacean, sending up "rooster tails" of spray when going at top speed. It lives in coastal and deep oceanic waters of the northern Pacific and is not known to migrate. It eats small fish and squid.

Dall's porpoise (*Phocoenoides dalli*) 6 ft.

DEEP-CRESTED WHALE—*See* ANDREW'S BEAKED WHALE.

DELPHINIDAE (Oceanic Dolphins)—A family of toothed whales with sharp, cone-shaped teeth in both upper and lower jaws. They range in size from 4.5 feet to the killer whale's thirty feet. Most have a slender, beaklike snout; a bulging forehead; a single crescent-shaped blowhole; and a well-developed, hooked dorsal fin. They have streamlined bodies; large, tapering flippers; and deeply notched flukes. They are the most abundant of all cetaceans. More than thirty species—including the killer whale, false killer whale, and pilot whales—are found in every ocean and sea. They display a great variety of color patterns—stripes, bands, and spots. These intelligent, playful, and affectionate cetaceans feed on fish and squid.

DENSE-BEAKED WHALE—*See* BLAINVILLE'S BEAKED WHALE.

DOLPHINS—A group of small toothed whales that live in both fresh and salt water. *See* DELPHINIDAE and PLATANISTIDAE.

DUSKY DOLPHIN *(Lagenorhynchus obscurus)*—An odontocete of the Delphinidae family. This six-foot, 250-pound oceanic dolphin is quite similar to the Pacific white-sided dolphin. It has a very short beak; 144 sharp teeth; and a tall, slightly hooked dorsal fin. Its color pattern is complex. The overall body, tail, and snout are bluish black, with pale gray bands on the sides and bars on the back. The curved flippers are light gray. Newborns are two feet long. The dusky dolphin lives inshore in all temperate waters of the southern hemisphere and travels in groups of hundreds. It eats fish and squid, cooperating with other dolphins to herd them to the surface where they are easily caught. These friendly, fast-swimming dolphins often bow-ride.

dusky dolphin (*Lagenorhynchus obscurus*) 6 ft.

DWARF SPERM WHALE *(Kogia simus)*—An odontocete of the Physeteridae family. This short, robust 8.5-foot, 340-pound sperm whale is similar to the pygmy sperm but is smaller and has a shorter snout. Its larger, more erect dorsal fin resembles that of the bottlenose dolphin. Its single blowhole is set well back from the tip of the squarish snout. The lower jaw is well behind the snout tip and contains twenty-two teeth. There may be several short pleats on the throat. This whale is dark steel gray above, with lighter sides and a white belly. A gray bracket mark behind the head looks like a gill. The flukes are deeply notched. Newborns are 3.3 feet long. This whale lives in temperate and tropical oceans worldwide, both inshore and offshore. Scientists do not know if the dwarf sperm whale migrates. It eats squid, fish, and crustaceans, diving at least three hundred feet to feed.

dwarf sperm whale *(Kogia simus)* 8.5 ft.

ESCHRICHTIIDAE (Gray Whales)—A family of bottom-feeding baleen whales. Eschrichtiidae (es-krik-TEE-eh-dee) have short baleen and a series of knuckles or humps along the tail stock instead of a dorsal fin. Although these forty-five-foot whales are now found only in the North Pacific, they once lived in the Atlantic too. Only one living species of this family is known. *See* GRAY WHALE.

ESTUARINE DOLPHIN—*See* TUCUXI DOLPHIN.

FALSE KILLER WHALE *(Pseudorca crassidens)*—An odontocete of the Delphinidae family. This eighteen-foot, 2.5-ton oceanic dolphin is one of the largest dolphins. Compared to its long, slender body, its narrow, smoothly tapered head is small. The rounded, bulging forehead overhangs the lower jaw, and forty-four large, strong teeth line the beakless jaws. This whale has a tall, hooked dorsal fin just behind midback and broad, curved flippers. It is all black except for gray on the chest and flippers. Newborns are five feet long. The false killer whale lives in warm temperate and tropical waters around the world, often in herds of one hundred or more, rarely approaching land. It eats squid and large fish. This is the largest whale known to bow-ride. In captivity it is easily trained.

false killer whale (*Pseudorca crassidens*) 18 ft.

fin whale calf

FIN WHALE *(Balaenoptera physalus)*—Also called common rorqual. A mysticete of the Balaenopteridae family. This seventy-foot, fifty-ton rorqual whale is the second largest cetacean, and the slimmest. The twenty-two-foot newborns weigh four tons. A prominent ridge runs down the middle of the long, narrow, flat-topped snout. Hair grows along both jaws, with a beardlike bunch on the tip of the lower jaw. Up to eighty long pleats on the throat expand to allow larger mouthfuls of small fish, squid, krill, and other invertebrates. Seven hundred yellow-and-gray-striped baleen plates that are three feet long line the upper jaw. The flippers are relatively small; the hooked, two-foot-tall dorsal fin sits far back; and the very broad flukes are about one-fourth as wide as the body is long. The back and sides are

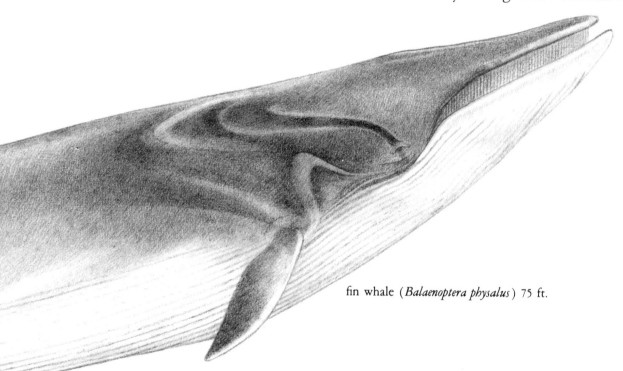

fin whale (*Balaenoptera physalus*) 75 ft.

brownish black, with grayish white V-shaped patches just behind the head. The belly is white. The lower left jaw is black, but the lower right is white. This whale's spout is cone-shaped and is twenty feet high. Fin whales are the most common of the baleen whales and live throughout the world in all oceans, although their range is not quite as far north as that of some whales. They feed in polar areas, migrating toward the equator and toward shore in winter. They travel up to twelve thousand miles in a year. They are among the fastest swimmers of the great whales.

FINLESS PORPOISE *(Neophocaena phocaenoides)*—An odontocete of Phocoenidae family. This shy six-foot, one-hundred-pound porpoise has fifty-two spade-shaped teeth. It eats squid, shrimp, prawns, and small fish and sometimes joins others of its species to surround schools of fish. This porpoise looks somewhat like a beluga, but it is smaller. Its color varies from almost white to black. It has a beakless head with a steep, rounded melon and deeply notched flukes. Instead of a dorsal fin, it has a series of bumps three to four inches high along its back. Mothers carry their twenty-two-inch babies on their backs. The bumps may help the young stay on. This whale lives in shallow water along the coasts and river mouths of Japan and southern Asia and is sometimes found in rivers with Chinese river dolphins.

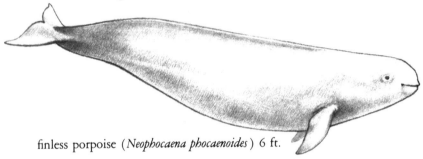

finless porpoise *(Neophocaena phocaenoides)* 6 ft.

FRANCISCANA DOLPHIN *(Pontoporia blainvillei)*—Also called La Plata River dolphin. An odontocete of the Platanistidae family. This five-foot, eighty-pound dolphin resembles river dolphins but is not known to live in fresh water. It inhabits shallow waters off the coasts of Uruguay and Argentina, especially near the mouth of the La Plata River. It has an extremely long, slender beak that is longer, in proportion to body length, than that of any other dolphin. It has 220 slender, sharp teeth—only the spinner dolphin has more. Its eyes are small but well developed. The flippers are broad and bladelike with serrated back edges. The tall, rounded, slightly hooked dorsal fin sits near midback. The flukes are notched. The back is gray and the belly is a soft buff. Newborns are twenty inches long. The franciscana dolphin probes the muddy bottom for fish, squid, octopus, and shrimp with its long, slender beak.

franciscana dolphin *(Pontoporia blainvillei)* 5 ft.

FRASER'S DOLPHIN (*Lagenodelphis hosei*)—Also called short-snouted dolphin.

An odontocete of the Delphinidae family. This robust 7.5-foot, two-hundred-pound oceanic dolphin has a short beak; 160 slender, pointed teeth; slightly notched flukes; and a small, slightly hooked dorsal fin. The back is bluish gray and the belly is white. Three long pale gray and dark gray stripes run along the sides. Newborns are about three feet long. Fraser's dolphin lives, sometimes in groups of thousands, in deep temperate and tropical waters throughout the world. This deep-diver eats squid and crustaceans.

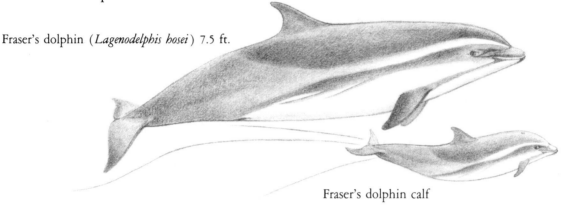

Fraser's dolphin (*Lagenodelphis hosei*) 7.5 ft.

Fraser's dolphin calf

GANGES RIVER DOLPHIN (*Platanista gangetica*)—Also called Ganges susu.

An odontocete of the Platanistidae family. Some people think that this five-foot, seventy-seven-pound river dolphin is the same as the Indus River dolphin. It has the same robust body and is about the same size and shape. The small head has a narrow eighteen-inch-long beak with 120 sharply pointed teeth, and a bulbous forehead. This dolphin has extremely broad, flat flippers; broad, notched flukes; and a low ridge along the back instead of a dorsal fin. Its eyes are reduced to pinholes, and it can see only to distinguish between dark and light. But like the other Platanistidae, it uses sonar to locate shrimp and fish. The color is dull black or medium gray, grading to light gray on the belly. Newborns are thirty inches long. The Ganges River dolphin lives in all parts of the Ganges River drainage system but does not go into the open sea.

Ganges River dolphin (*Platanista gangetica*) 5 ft.

GANGES SUSU—*See* GANGES RIVER DOLPHIN.

GERVAIS'S BEAKED WHALE—*See* GULF STREAM BEAKED WHALE.

GIANT BOTTLENOSE WHALE—*See* BAIRD'S BEAKED WHALE.

GINKGO-TOOTHED BEAKED WHALE *(Mesoplodon ginkgodens)*—Also called Japanese beaked whale. An odontocete of the Ziphiidae family. A living specimen of this seventeen-foot, 1.7-ton beaked whale has never been seen, and its color is not known for sure. When dead, it is black with a white belly. It has a streamlined body; short narrow flippers; very wide, unnotched flukes; and very narrow, pointed jaws. Males have two enormous teeth in the lower jaw. These four-inch-long, four-inch-wide teeth—the widest cetacean teeth known—are shaped like the leaf of a ginkgo tree and are set close to the middle of the beak. This whale lives only in warm tropical and temperate waters of the North Pacific and the northern Indian Ocean. It probably eats fish and squid.

tooth 4 in. by 4 in.

ginkgo-toothed beaked whale *(Mesoplodon ginkgodens)* 17 ft.

GOOSE BEAKED WHALE—*See* CUVIER'S BEAKED WHALE.

GRAMPUS—*See* RISSO'S DOLPHIN.

GRAY DOLPHIN— *See* RISSO'S DOLPHIN.

GRAY WHALE *(Eschrichtius robustus)*—A mysticete of the Eschrichtiidae family. This forty-five-foot, forty-five-ton whale may be the best-known baleen whale. It has up to 360 short, coarse, yellowish white baleen plates. The narrow, triangular head is ten feet long. Many small hairs grow on the top jaw, and up to 120 bristles line the lower jaw. This whale has two to four deep throat pleats, long flippers, and a low hump followed by a series of knobs or knuckles instead of a dorsal fin. The enormous flukes are twelve feet across. This whale is mottled gray. Its puffy, geyser-shaped spout is ten to fifteen feet high. It lives only in the northern Pacific Ocean. Following coastal waters, it migrates from its summer feeding grounds in the Chukchi and Bering seas to its breeding and calving areas off Baja California. This thirteen-thousand-mile annual trip is the longest known migration of any mammal. Of all cetaceans, mother gray whales are among the most protective of their fifteen-foot calves. Unlike most baleen whales, the gray whale is a bottom-feeder, plowing along the muddy bottom for krill. As an adaptation for this method of feeding, the baleen on the right side is shorter than that on the left.

gray whale *(Eschrichtius robustus)* 45 ft.

GRAY WHALES—A family of baleen whales. *See* ESCHRICHTIIDAE.

GRAY'S BEAKED WHALE *(Mesoplodon grayi)*—Also called scamperdown whale. An odontocete of the Ziphiidae family. This fourteen-foot, one-ton toothed whale is the smallest of the beaked whales. It has a slender body, a small head, a small melon, and a long, narrow beak. Adult males have two large triangular teeth in the lower jaw, well behind the tip. They also may have forty-four small teeth—twenty-two on each side of the upper jaw. The flippers are short and wide. The dorsal fin is sharply pointed. Newborns are less than eight feet long. This whale is known mostly from stranded animals. It seems to live in all temperate waters of the South Pacific and Indian oceans. It has also been found in the Netherlands.

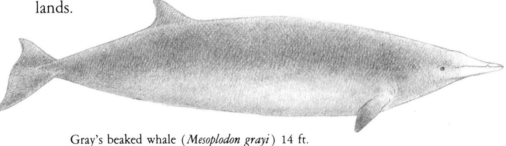

Gray's beaked whale (*Mesoplodon grayi*) 14 ft.

GREENLAND RIGHT WHALE—*See* BOWHEAD WHALE.

GULF PORPOISE *(Phocoena sinus)*—Also called cochito and vaquita. An odontocete of the Phocoenidae family. Until recently, almost nothing was known about this 4.5-foot, eighty-pound porpoise. Only stranded or netted animals had been seen. This bottom-feeder has seventy-eight small, spade-shaped teeth in its blunt snout. It eats fish and squid. Its back is medium gray, and its belly is white. The low, triangular dorsal fin is higher than that of the common porpoise, and the flippers are larger. The gulf porpoise is thought to live only in shallow water in the upper Sea of Cortez (Gulf of California).

gulf porpoise (*Phocoena sinus*) 4.5 ft.

GULF STREAM BEAKED WHALE *(Mesoplodon europaeus)*—Also

called Antillean beaked whale and Gervais's beaked whale. An odontocete of the Ziphiidae family. This twenty-two-foot, three-ton whale has a very small head with a slender beak. The back and sides are dark bluish gray grading to light on the underside, with irregular white markings on the belly. Adult males have two four-inch triangular teeth that protrude at an angle from the middle of the lower jaw. This whale has unnotched flukes and low-set flippers. Newborn calves are 7.5 feet long. The Gulf Stream beaked whale has never been seen alive. It is known only from strandings along the shores of warm temperate and subtropical waters of the Atlantic. It eats squid.

Gulf Stream beaked whale *(Mesoplodon europaeus)* 22 ft.

HARBOR PORPOISE *(Phocoena phocoena)*—Also called common porpoise.

An odontocete of the Phocoenidae family. This chunky, ninety-pound, 4.5-foot porpoise is one of the smallest whales. It has a small, rounded head with a sloping forehead and no beak; 152 small, spade-shaped teeth; and deeply notched flukes. The triangular dorsal fin and short, rounded flippers occasionally have blunt bumps on the rear edges. The back is usually dark gray or black, fading to lighter gray on the sides and white on the belly. Newborns are thirty inches long. This porpoise lives in cold temperate and sub-Arctic waters of the northern hemisphere. It is usually seen near coastal bays and rivermouths. It is the cetacean most often seen in European waters. Large schools migrate inshore and offshore according to the availability of food and ice-free water. The harbor porpoise eats fish, shrimp, octopus, and squid.

harbor porpoise *(Phocoena phocoena)* 4.5 ft.

HEAVISIDE'S DOLPHIN *(Cephalorhynchus heavisidii)*—Also called Benguela dolphin. An odontocete of the Delphinidae family. Very little is known about this rare, shy 4.5-foot, eighty-eight-pound oceanic dolphin. Its broad, flat head has a gently sloping forehead, a very short snout with the lower jaw extending beyond the upper, and 120 small, pointed teeth. Its back is black, its stomach white. Three lobes of white extend up onto the sides. It has a low, triangular dorsal fin; narrow, egg-shaped flippers; and notched flukes. It lives only in the cold water of the Benguela Current off the west coast of South Africa. Heaviside's dolphin eats squid and probably bottom-dwelling fish.

Heaviside's dolphin (*Cephalorhynchus heavisidii*) 4.5 ft.

HECTOR'S BEAKED WHALE *(Mesoplodon hectori)*—Also called skew beaked whale. An odontocete of the Ziphiidae family. This fourteen-foot whale is known from only a few specimens. It probably lives in temperate waters of the southern hemisphere. It is dark on the back and pale gray on the belly. The slightly notched flukes are white underneath. Males have two relatively small, triangular teeth near the tip of the lower jaw of the short beak.

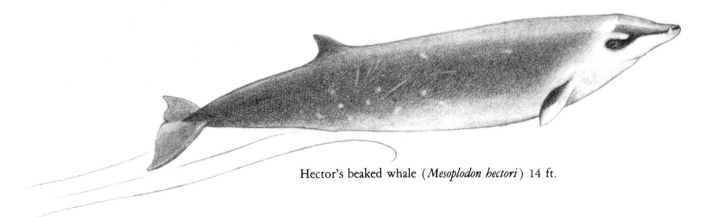

Hector's beaked whale (*Mesoplodon hectori*) 14 ft.

HECTOR'S DOLPHIN *(Cephalorhynchus hectori)*—Also called New Zealand's dolphin. An odontocete of the Delphinidae family. This five-foot, eighty-eight-pound oceanic dolphin lives in coastal waters near the shores of New Zealand. Some of these dolphins have become famous for their friendship with children. Hector's dolphin has a slight beak, a slanted mouth, and 128 teeth. The dorsal fin and small flippers are rounded. The flukes have a shallow notch. The color pattern is complex. The sides of the head, flippers, dorsal fin, and tail are black; the belly, lower jaw, and throat are white; and the back is medium to dark gray. Fingers of white run into the sides, and patches of gray adorn the forehead. This dolphin eats shellfish, shrimp, and small fish.

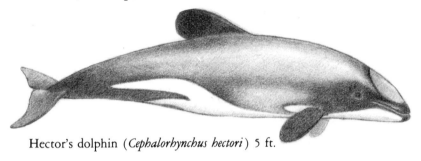

Hector's dolphin (*Cephalorhynchus hectori*) 5 ft.

HELMET DOLPHIN—*See* CLYMENE DOLPHIN.

HOOKED-FIN DOLPHIN—*See* PACIFIC WHITE-SIDED DOLPHIN.

HOURGLASS DOLPHIN *(Lagenorhynchus cruciger)*—An odontocete of the Delphinidae family. This robust six-foot, 220-pound oceanic dolphin is strikingly colored, with a black-and-white hourglass pattern on its sides. The snout, flippers, dorsal fin, flukes, and back are black. The throat, belly, and sides of the face are white. The hourglass dolphin has a tall, sharply hooked dorsal fin; long, narrow flippers; a short, thick beak; and 112 pointed teeth. This little-known dolphin lives only in deep water of the Antarctic and sub-Antarctic oceans and is the only dolphin found in the ice pack of the Antarctic. Its winters are spent near the tip of South America. It eats fairly large fish. This acrobatic cetacean leaps, spins, and bow-rides.

hourglass dolphin (*Lagenorhynchus cruciger*) 6 ft.

HUBB'S BEAKED WHALE *(Mesoplodon carlhubbsi)*—Also called arch

beaked whale. An odontocete of the Ziphiidae family. This robust, seventeen-foot beaked whale is quite similar to Andrew's beaked whale and may be the same species. It has never been seen alive. It has a narrow tail and a small head with a well-defined beak. Males have two massive teeth—6.3 inches tall, three inches wide, and two inches thick—that protrude from the lower jaw. The small, slim flippers fit into pockets on the animal's sides when pressed against the body. The flukes are unnotched. The body is dark gray to black with a white bump or "beanie" just in front of the blowhole. In males, the front half of the lower jaw is white. Newborns are eight feet long. This whale lives in cold temperate waters of the north Pacific. It probably eats squid and fish.

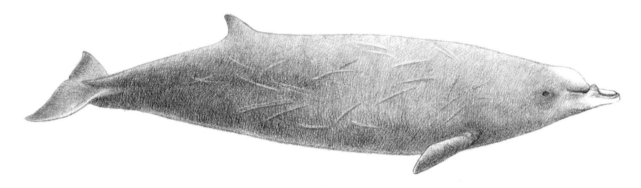

Hubbs' beaked whale (*Mesoplodon carlhubbsi*) 17 ft.

Hubbs' beaked whale calf

HUMPBACK WHALE *(Megaptera novaeangliae)*—A mysticete of the Balaenopteridae family. This fifty-foot, forty-five-ton rorqual whale is best known for its complicated mating songs. The humpback's huge head, which resembles that of an alligator, does not have a ridge down the middle as do the heads of other rorquals. It has a rounded projection on the tip of the lower jaw. A string of fleshy knobs containing coarse hairs adorn the upper and lower jaws. The humpback has many long, widely spaced throat pleats and up to eight hundred baleen plates that are twenty-five inches long in the upper jaw. The plates are generally black,

humpback whale (*Megaptera novaeangliae*) 50 ft.

with olive-black bristles. The humpback's enormous, scalloped flippers are nearly one-third as long as its body. The eighteen-foot, butterfly-shaped flukes are broader than those of any other whale. Their rear edges are serrated and deeply notched. The tiny, sharply hooked dorsal fin is set well past midback. This whale is basically black or gray, with white on the throat, belly, flippers, and undersides of the flukes. Its bushy ten-foot spout is shaped like an upside-down pear. Newborns are about fifteen feet long. The humpback whale lives in all oceans in both tropical and polar waters. It makes extensive migrations from summer polar feeding grounds to warm breeding areas in winter. This whale eats 1.5 tons per day of krill and schooling fish, which it often traps with a bubble net (see description on page 27). This slow swimmer is one of the most acrobatic of the large whales. Humpbacks are now rare and are completely protected by international law.

INDO-PACIFIC BEAKED WHALE *(Mesoplodon pacificus)*—Also

called Longman's beaked whale. An odontocete of the Ziphiidae family. This whale is the least known of all cetaceans. It is known only from two skulls that were found in Queensland, Australia, and Somalia, Africa. It probably lives only in tropical waters. Scientists have no idea what it looks like, but it must be one of the largest of the beaked whales. One skull was four feet long, which suggests an animal twenty-three to twenty-five feet long. It had one pair of teeth at the end of the lower jaw.

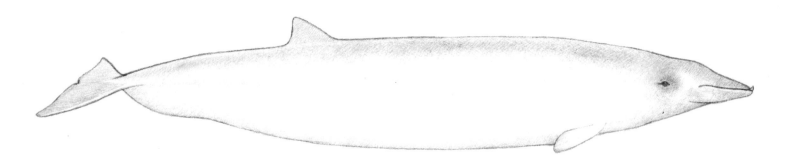

Indo-Pacific beaked whale *(Mesoplodon pacificus)* ?23–25 ft.

INDO-PACIFIC HUMP-BACKED DOLPHIN (*Sousa chinensis*)—An odontocete of the Delphinidae family. This shy 6.5-foot, 180-pound oceanic dolphin is not well known. It is found only in shallow inshore waters of warm temperate and tropical seas throughout the Indo-Pacific area. It has 120 sharply pointed teeth; a long cylindrical beak; short, rounded flippers; and notched flukes. The small, hooked, triangular dorsal fin sits on a broad base at midback. The color is deep gray to ivory white, spotted with a variety of patterns. Newborns are thirty-five inches long. This dolphin eats fish.

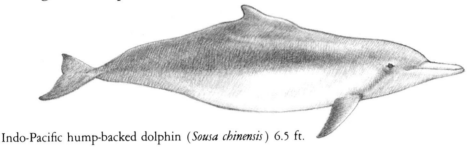

Indo-Pacific hump-backed dolphin (*Sousa chinensis*) 6.5 ft.

INDUS RIVER DOLPHIN (*Platanista minor*)—Also called Indus susu. An odontocete of the Platanistidae family. This five-foot river dolphin may be the same as (or a subspecies of) the Ganges River dolphin. It differs from that dolphin only in its geographical location and in having a bony crest on the skull. It is found only in a small part of the Indus River. This dolphin is blind; its pinhole eyes have no lenses. It has up to 132 sharply pointed teeth. It eats fish and crustaceans. It has a long, narrow beak, slightly thickened at the tip; notched flukes; and broad bladelike flippers. The dorsal fin is replaced by a small triangular hump. Newborns are twenty-eight inches long. This whale is either extinct or in danger of becoming extinct within the next few years.

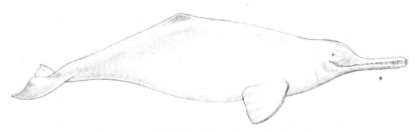

Indus River dolphin (*Platanista minor*) 5 ft.

INDUS SUSU—*See* INDUS RIVER DOLPHIN.

IRRAWADDY DOLPHIN *(Orcaella brevirostris)*—Also called snubfin.

An odontocete of the Delphinidae family. This 6.5-foot, 220-pound oceanic dolphin is similar to the beluga in general body form. It has a large, bulging forehead but almost no beak. The flippers are broad and long, with a blunt or rounded tip. The small, curved dorsal fin is slightly behind midback. The flukes are notched. The color is generally gray to dark slate blue, lighter on the belly. Newborns are twenty-five inches long. The Irrawaddy dolphin lives in tropical Indo-Pacific waters close to shore, often going into rivers. It eats fish and crustaceans and is probably a bottom-feeder. Local fishermen say it drives fish into their nets.

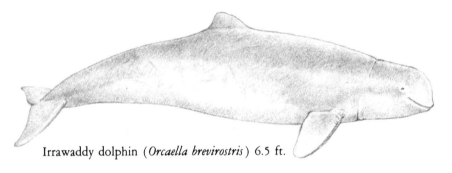

Irrawaddy dolphin *(Orcaella brevirostris)* 6.5 ft.

JAPANESE BEAKED WHALE—*See* GINKGO-TOOTHED BEAKED WHALE.

KILLER WHALE *(Orcinus orca)*—Also called blackfish and orca. An odontocete of the Delphinidae family. This thirty-foot, eight-ton oceanic dolphin is the only cetacean that regularly eats mammalian prey. Like a wolf, this clever predator hunts in packs. It eats almost anything—other cetaceans, seals, squid, penguins, sea turtles, sharks, and fish. However, there is no record of its ever attacking a human. This heavy-bodied whale has a broad, conical head with a very indistinct beak. Its big mouth is filled with forty-eight large, backward-curved, conical teeth that can tear chunks of flesh from a blue whale. It has deeply notched flukes, a six-foot dorsal fin that is hooked like that of a shark, and enormous, broad, paddle-shaped flippers. It is shiny black with white patches above and behind the eyes, on the stomach, up into the sides, and on the chin, the throat,

and the underside of the flukes. The color pattern varies from one killer whale to another, which makes it possible to identify individuals, pods, and populations. Newborns are eight feet long. Killer whales live in family groups of several hundred—remaining in them for life—in all oceans, mostly in cooler coastal waters. This extremely intelligent whale is gentle and tame and survives well in captivity.

killer whale (*Orcinus orca*) 30 ft.

The color pattern varies among individual killer whales.

LA PLATA RIVER DOLPHIN—*See* FRANCISCANA DOLPHIN.

LONG-FINNED PILOT WHALE *(Globicephala melaena)*—Also called

caa'ing whale and pothead whale. An odontocete of the Delphinidae family. This twenty-foot, four-ton oceanic dolphin has a long, slender body; a thick, bulbous forehead that resembles an inverted iron pot; and only the slightest hint of a beak. It has forty-eight peglike teeth, deeply notched flukes, and a broad, hooked dorsal fin set far forward on its back. Its sickle-shaped flippers are one-fifth as long as its body. Newborns are six feet long. This whale is slate gray to black, with an anchor-shaped patch of grayish white on the throat and stomach and sometimes behind the dorsal fin and eye. It lives in pods of several hundred in temperate and subpolar waters of all oceans except the North Pacific, although it lived there until the late eighteenth century. Compact schools follow one leader when traveling, staying in tight formation like geese. This whale can dive thirty-three hundred feet or more and can stay underwater for up to two hours. It eats fish and squid. The pilot whale is a quick learner and is often kept in captivity.

long-finned pilot whale (*Globicephala melaena*) 20 ft.

LONGMAN'S BEAKED WHALE—*See* INDO-PACIFIC BEAKED WHALE.

LONG-SNOUTED SPINNER DOLPHIN—*See* SPINNER DOLPHIN.

MELON-HEADED WHALE *(Peponocephala electra)*—An odontocete of

the Delphinidae family. This 7.5-foot, 350-pound oceanic dolphin is a fast swimmer. It strongly resembles the pygmy killer whale. Its triangular head is quite unlike those of most dolphins—it has a rounded melon but no beak—and its body is longer and more slender. It has long, slim, gently curved flippers; a long, hooked dorsal fin like that of a shark; and one hundred sharply pointed teeth. Its back and sides are black; its throat and belly are slightly lighter, with white or light gray spots. The lips are white. The size of newborns is unknown. This rare whale eats squid and small fish. It lives in large herds in deep tropical and subtropical waters throughout the world.

melon-headed whale *(Peponocephala electra)* 7.5 ft.

MINKE WHALE *(Balaenoptera acutorostrata)*—Also called piked whale. A

mysticete of the Balaenopteridae family. This twenty-five-foot, eight-ton whale is the smallest of the rorqual whales. Females are larger than males, and newborn calves are ten feet long. The minke (MINK-ee) has a slender, extremely streamlined body; a flat, narrow, pointed snout with a single ridge running down the center; up to seventy long throat pleats; and long, slim flippers. The broad, notched flukes are about one-fourth the body length. The tall, hooked dorsal fin is located near the tail. The 720 yellowish baleen plates are twelve inches long and five inches wide. The spout is low and plume-shaped. This whale's back is black to dark gray, and its belly and the underside of the flippers are white. The minke gulps krill, copepods, and shoaling fish, breaching to scare them into compact groups. It lives in open seas worldwide, congregating in schools of several hundred to feed in polar seas and migrating to tropical seas to calve. It goes closer to the ice pack than any other baleen whale. It is the last of the great whales to be commercially fished.

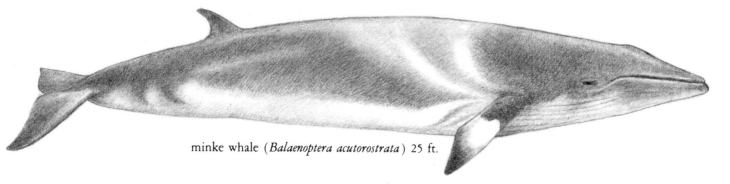

minke whale *(Balaenoptera acutorostrata)* 25 ft.

MONODONTIDAE (White Whales)—A family of toothed whales that includes only two species, the beluga and the narwhal. These medium-sized whales are found only in the Arctic. They have long bodies, rounded foreheads, and a neck line, but no throat pleats or dorsal fins. Their flippers are short, broad, and rounded. Adults are white, calves are darker.

MYSTICETI (Baleen Whales)—One of the two orders of whales living today. It includes the largest animal that ever lived. This group has three families—the Balaenidae (right whales), the Balaenopteridae (rorqual whales), and the Eschrichtiidae (gray whales)—and ten species. These whales have paired blowholes on top of their heads and baleen instead of teeth. The baleen is a special adaptation for straining small schooling fish and zooplankton from the ocean. Baleen whales move through the sea with open jaws, taking in enormous mouthfuls of food and seawater. The water escapes through the horny bristles of the baleen, but the zooplankton and small fish are trapped inside the mouth. Most baleen whales have accordionlike pleats on their throats. These whales range in size from sixteen to one hundred feet long. Females are usually longer than males. The spout is usually very distinct. Most baleen whales migrate from the polar feeding areas to warm tropical waters to calve. They are found in most seas.

NARWHAL *(Monodon monoceros)*—Also called unicorn whale. An odontocete of the Monodontidae family. The fifteen-foot, 1.8-ton narwhal (NAR-wall) is quite similar to the beluga in appearance. It has the same cylindrical body and a small, blunt head with a bulbous forehead, slight beak, and small mouth. But its teeth are unique. All narwhals have two teeth embedded in the upper jaw. In adult males the left tooth grows through the upper lip and forms a left-handed spiraling tusk unlike that of any other animal. This amazing tooth may be nine feet long and weigh twenty pounds. No one knows its purpose, though it may be used in dueling for mates. This whale has no dorsal fin, but an uneven two-inch-high ridge runs from midback to the fan-shaped, deeply notched flukes. The short flippers have upturned tips. The spout is low and indistinct. The five-foot newborn calves are blotchy slate gray. Adults have white streaks and patches on the belly and sides. Old males are almost completely white. Narwhals live only in the Arctic—in pods of twenty or fewer—in deep water in winter and near shore or in bays close to the pack ice in summer. They are among the most northerly cetaceans. They eat squid, fish, crab, and shrimp. Eskimos hunt them for their tusks and for food.

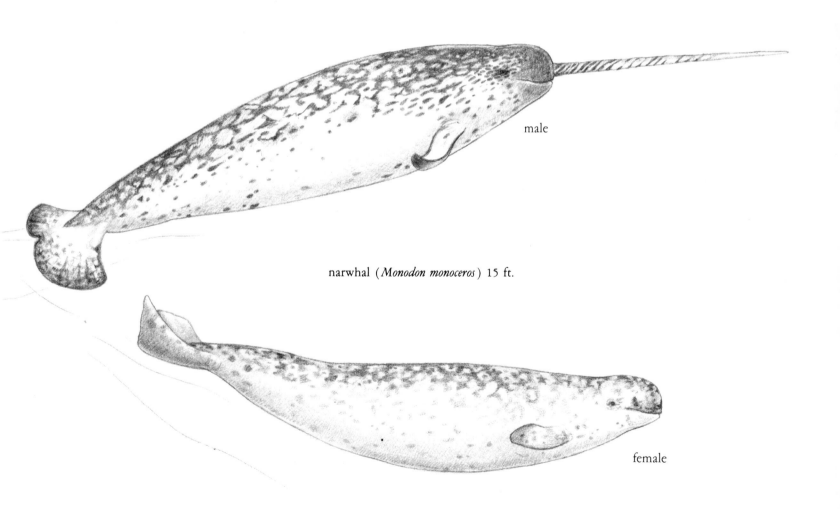

male

narwhal (*Monodon monoceros*) 15 ft.

female

NEW ZEALAND'S DOLPHIN—*See* HECTOR'S DOLPHIN.

NORTHERN BOTTLENOSE WHALE (*Hyperoodon ampullatus*)—

An odontocete of the Ziphiidae family. This heavyset thirty-foot, four-ton whale is one of the best known of the beaked whales. The head has a bulbous melon and a beak similar to that of the bottlenose dolphin but much larger. The flippers are small and narrow; the flukes are un-notched. Adult males have two two-inch teeth at the tip of the lower jaw. The bushy spout is 6.5 feet high. The back is normally dark, grading to smoky gray on the belly. Newborns are ten feet long. This whale eats squid and herring. In summer it lives in deep offshore Arctic waters, migrating to cold temperate waters of the North Atlantic in winter. It is one of the deepest divers among cetaceans, going down to 7,900 feet and staying underwater for two hours. Members of a pod will not desert a wounded member, and this helped whalers destroy large numbers for their oil. This whale has been almost wiped out.

northern bottlenose whale (*Hyperoodon ampullatus*) 30 ft.

NORTHERN FOURTOOTH WHALE—*See* BAIRD'S BEAKED WHALE.

NORTHERN RIGHT WHALE—*See* RIGHT WHALE.

NORTHERN RIGHT WHALE DOLPHIN *(Lissodelphis borealis)*—An odontocete of the Delphinidae family. This ten-foot, 154-pound oceanic dolphin doesn't have a dorsal fin. It is the slimmest of all dolphins. The melon slopes gently to a small, slender beak. This whale has 196 small, pointed teeth; slim, pointed flippers; and very narrow, graceful-ly curved, deeply notched flukes. It is black but has a striking pure white pattern on the belly, from the chest to the undersides of the flukes. New-borns are forty inches long. This fast swimmer bow-rides gray whales but usually shuns humans and boats. It eats squid and fish. It lives only in deep temperate waters of the North Pacific, migrating southward in winter and northward in summer.

northern right whale dolphin (*Lissodelphis borealis*) 10 ft.

NORTH SEA BEAKED WHALE—*See* SOWERBY'S BEAKED WHALE.

OCEANIC DOLPHINS—*See* DELPHINIDAE.

ODONTOCETI (Toothed Whales)—One of the two orders of whales that are living today. All Odontoceti have teeth at least during some stage of their lives. Some have as many as 240 teeth, others as few as 1. But they have only one set in a lifetime. In some species the teeth remain buried in the gums of all individuals except adult males. Different species of Odonto-ceti can be identified by the number, position, or shape of the teeth (most are cone-shaped). There are sixty-six species in this group, which includes the dolphins and porpoises. Every toothed whale has paired nares (nos-trils), but only a single blowhole. The blowhole is set slightly off center on top of the head, except in the sperm whale, which has its blowhole at the tip of its snout. Toothed whales live in all oceans of the world and range in length from 4.5 to 60 feet. Most eat fish, squid, and shellfish. There are six families of Odontoceti: Delphinidae (oceanic dolphins), Monodontidae (white whales), Phocoenidae (porpoises), Physeteridae (sperm whales), Platanistidae (river dolphins), and Ziphiidae (beaked whales).

ORCA—*See* KILLER WHALE.

PACIFIC SPOTTED DOLPHIN—*See* BRIDLED SPOTTED DOLPHIN.

PACIFIC WHITE-SIDED DOLPHIN *(Lagenorhynchus obliquidens)*—Also called hooked-fin dolphin and white-striped dolphin. An odontocete of the Delphinidae family. This 7.5-foot, 150-pound oceanic dolphin has a short, thick beak and 120 small, sharp teeth. The curved flippers and notched flukes are black on the front and pale gray on the rear. The beak and back are black. A black stripe separates the light gray sides from the pearly white belly. A pair of white stripes curve from the top of the head almost to the tail. Newborns are three feet long. This acrobatic fast swimmer spins on its axis while making tremendous leaps. Family groups and huge schools of thousands inhabit offshore waters of the temperate North Pacific. In winter some move to warmer inshore waters to calve. This dolphin eats fish and squid.

Pacific white-sided dolphin (*Lagenorhynchus obliquidens*) 7.5 ft.

PEALE'S DOLPHIN *(Lagenorhynchus australis)*—Also called blackfin dolphin. An odontocete of the Delphinidae family. Little is known about this friendly seven-foot, 250-pound oceanic dolphin. It has 120 teeth. It is dark gray with a white belly. The face and throat are black, and two side patches are gray. The large, hooked dorsal fin, small flippers, and notched flukes are dark-colored. This dolphin is a bottom-feeder and is especially fond of octopus. It lives in family groups of up to fifty and is found only in coastal waters near the tip of South America and the Falkland Islands.

Peale's dolphin (*Lagenorhynchus australis*) 7 ft.

PHOCOENIDAE (Porpoises)—A family of toothed whales that includes all very small beakless whales with spade-shaped teeth (flattened at the crown), rounded foreheads, and either small, triangular dorsal fins or none at all. They range from 4.5 to 6 feet long. Most live in cooler coastal waters of the North Atlantic and Pacific oceans. A few are found around South America and the southern tip of Africa. There are six species in this family: Burmeister's porpoise, Dall's porpoise, finless porpoise, gulf porpoise, harbor porpoise, and spectacled porpoise.

PHYSETERIDAE (Sperm Whales)—A family of toothed whales that have a large spermaceti organ (case filled with oil) in the head, above the upper jaw. Their enormous heads are up to one-third of their body length. The lower jaw is underslung and has large cone-shaped teeth that fit into sockets in the toothless upper jaw when the mouth is closed. This family ranges in size from 8.5 to 60 feet and includes the largest of the toothed whales. Sperm whales live in all oceans of the world. There are three living species in this family: the sperm whale, dwarf sperm whale, and pygmy sperm whale. The last two have dorsal fins and a blowhole that is on top of the head. The first has no dorsal fin, and its blowhole is at the tip of its snout.

PIEBALD DOLPHIN—*See* COMMERSON'S DOLPHIN.

PIKED WHALE—*See* MINKE WHALE.

PILOT WHALE—*See* LONG-FINNED PILOT WHALE *and* SHORT-FINNED PILOT WHALE.

PLATANISTIDAE (River Dolphins)—A family of toothed whales that live in five separate river systems of Asia and South America. They are 5 to 7.5 feet long and have very long, slender beaks, many small teeth, bulging foreheads, relatively low dorsal fins, and large broad flippers. Their neckline is noticeable, and the head can move freely. All but the Amazon River dolphin have poor vision, probably because of their muddy environments. This family has five species: Amazon River dolphin, Chinese River dolphin, franciscana dolphin, Ganges River dolphin, and Indus River dolphin.

PORPOISES—A group of small toothed whales. *See* PHOCOENIDAE.

POTHEAD WHALE—*See* LONG-FINNED PILOT WHALE.

PYGMY BLUE WHALE *(Balaenoptera musculus brevicauda)*—A seventy-two-foot subspecies of the blue whale. It is found in the Antarctic and off the Pacific coast of Central America, Mexico, and the United States. It is somewhat smaller than the ordinary blue whale and has larger baleen plates, a shorter tail, and a longer trunk. *See also* BLUE WHALE.

PYGMY KILLER WHALE *(Feresa attenuata)*—An odontocete of the Delphinidae family. This eight-foot, 375-pound oceanic dolphin has a smoothly rounded, beakless head like that of a killer whale and a slender body like that of a pilot whale. It has forty-eight teeth, small flippers, deeply notched flukes, and a low, hooked dorsal fin near midback. It is dark gray or black on the back and lighter gray on the sides, with white goatee and lips and small white patches on the belly. Newborns are thirty inches long. This fish-eater lives in all tropical waters of the world. It may be more aggressive than the killer whale. In captivity it is very hostile toward humans.

pygmy killer whale (*Feresa attenuata*) 8 ft.

pygmy blue whale (*Balaenoptera musculus brevicauda*) 72 ft.

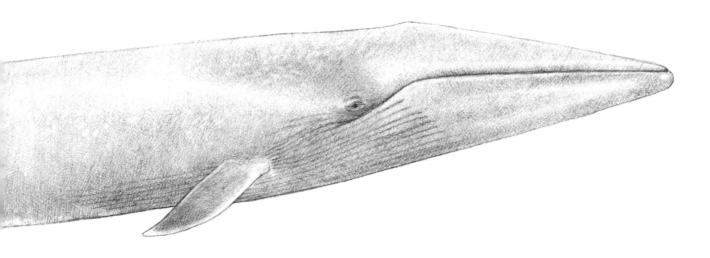

PYGMY RIGHT WHALE *(Caperea marginata)*—A mysticete of the Balaenidae family. This sixteen-foot, five-ton right whale is the smallest of the baleen whales. The huge head is one-fourth of the total body length. The lower jaw is arched, and the throat has two long pleats like those of the rorquals. The upper jaw is lined with 460 twenty-five-inch strips of yellowish white baleen. The body is more slender than those of other right whales. This whale has a small, hooked dorsal fin set far back near the tail; small, narrow, rounded flippers; and broad, deeply notched flukes. The back is dark gray and the belly white. The lower jaw is lighter in color than the upper. Newborns may be 6.5 feet long. Only a few dozen specimens of the pygmy right whale are known. This rare whale spends little time on the surface and its spout is barely visible. It lives in temperate waters of the southern hemisphere. It eats zooplankton.

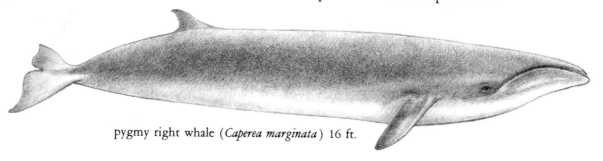

pygmy right whale (*Caperea marginata*) 16 ft.

PYGMY SPERM WHALE *(Kogia breviceps)*—An odontocete of the Physeteridae family. This twelve-foot, eight-hundred-pound whale is very similar to the dwarf sperm whale but is larger, has a smaller dorsal fin, and has more teeth. Its thirty-two thin, sharp, conical teeth appear in the lower jaw only. Its head resembles that of the sperm whale but is smaller. It has the smallest snout of all cetaceans. The tiny lower jaw sits well behind the snout tip, which gives this whale a sharklike appearance, as does the false gill mark on the sides of its head. The pygmy sperm whale has short, broad flippers; deeply notched flukes like those of a dolphin; and a short, stubby dorsal fin set far back. The back is dark bluish gray, shading to lighter gray on the sides and dull white on the belly. Many scars on males suggest fighting among themselves. Calves are four feet long. This whale is rarely seen and is not well known. Its spout is barely visible. It lives in nearly all tropical and temperate seas, mostly in deep offshore waters, but moves close to shore during calving season. A bottom-feeder, it eats squid, octopus, crab, fish, and shrimp.

pygmy sperm whale (*Kogia breviceps*) 12 ft.

right whale calf

RIGHT WHALE *(Eubalaena glacialis)*—A mysticete of the Balaenidae family. There are two distinct populations of right whales. Some consider the southern right whale to be a subspecies of the northern right whale *(E. glacialis australis);* others consider it a separate species *(E. australis).* They are quite similar. Both are fifty feet long and weigh sixty tons. Right whales have no dorsal fins, ridges, or throat grooves. The huge head is one-third of the body length. The enormous scooplike mouth has a highly arched lower jaw. The upper jaw is lined with six hundred narrow gray to black baleen plates that are seven feet long. The eighteen-foot babies are born with a series of crusty growths called callosities on the chin, on the lower lip, and above the eyes, and one called the bonnet on the top of the head near the blowhole. Numerous hairs grow in the callosities. Individual right whales can be identified by the sizes and shapes of these growths, which may be used as a defense, like the horn of a rhinoceros. A right whale's body is robust but very flexible—the head can almost touch the tail. Right whales have large, broad flippers and broad, smooth, deeply notched flukes. The two large blowholes are widely spaced, and the V-shaped spout is sixteen feet high. These whales are black to brown, with irregular white patches on the throat and belly. They live in small herds with strong social bonds and inhabit both cold and warm temperate regions worldwide. They are skim-feeders and eat zooplankton. They migrate from polar feeding grounds toward the equator in winter, often to shallow near-shore water of large bays. These whales have thick layers of blubber, which keep them afloat when killed. They are curious and will come close enough to humans to be touched, and they are slow swimmers. These characteristics made them easy for whalers to kill. They are now rare but are protected throughout the world.

right whale *(Eubalaena glacialis)* 50 ft.

RIGHT WHALES—A family of baleen whales. *See* BALAENIDAE.

RISSO'S DOLPHIN (*Grampus griseus*)—Also called grampus and gray dolphin. An odontocete of the Delphinidae family. This thirteen-foot, 660-pound oceanic dolphin has a bulbous melon but no beak. Its teeth are unusual for a dolphin. There are six to eight strong oval teeth at the front of the lower jaw, and none in the upper jaw. The robust body is similar to that of the pilot whale. The tall (twenty-inch), hooked dorsal fin sits at midback. The flukes and flippers are long and pointed. Adults are white or light gray, with dark dorsal fins, flippers, and flukes, and extensive scarring, probably from fighting with one another. The five-foot young are deep chocolate brown to almost black. Risso's dolphin lives in deep tropical and warm temperate waters around the world in groups of up to twenty-five and herds of several hundred. It eats squid and some fish. Pelorus Jack, the dolphin that accompanied steamships in New Zealand for twenty years, was a Risso's dolphin.

Risso's dolphin (*Grampus griseus*) 13 ft.

RIVER DOLPHINS—*See* PLATANISTIDAE.

RORQUAL WHALES—A family of baleen whales. *See* BALAENOPTERIDAE.

ROUGH-TOOTHED DOLPHIN *(Steno bredanensis)*—An odontocete

of the Delphinidae family. This ocean dolphin is eight feet long. The crowns of its 102 teeth are finely serrated instead of smooth and conical like those of other dolphins. The forehead slopes gently into the long, slender beak. The tall, hooked dorsal fin is the same shape as the flippers. This dolphin usually has a dark gray to purplish black back, with yellowish white to pink blotches on the sides and a white belly. The long, curved flippers and wide flukes are dark. Young are unknown. The rough-toothed dolphin lives in schools of fifty to several hundred offshore in tropical to warm temperate regions worldwide. It eats squid, octopus, and fish.

rough-toothed dolphin (*Steno bredanensis*) 8 ft.

SABER-TOOTHED BEAKED WHALE—*See* STEJNEGER'S BEAKED WHALE.

SCAMPERDOWN WHALE—*See* GRAY'S BEAKED WHALE.

SEA CANARY—*See* BELUGA.

SEI WHALE *(Balaenoptera borealis)*—A mysticete of the Balaenopteridae family. The snout of this sixty-foot, seventeen-ton rorqual is less rounded than that of the blue whale. Otherwise, the sei (SAY) has a typical flat-headed, streamlined rorqual body. A prominent ridge runs from the blow-hole to the tip of the snout, and a few hairs grow around the blowhole and on the tip of the lower jaw. This whale has up to sixty short throat pleats. Its 760 black baleen plates have white fringes and are twenty-six inches long. The flippers and flukes are shorter than those of other rorquals. The small, hooked dorsal fin sits well behind midback. The ten-foot-high spout is shaped like a cone. Newborn calves are fifteen feet long. This whale is the only rorqual that is a skim-feeder. It eats zooplankton, squid, and schooling fish. It can swim up to fifty miles per hour for short distances. It lives in temperate oceans worldwide, in both open seas and deep coastal waters. Some sei whales make long migrations from polar regions to warmer waters to calve. Sei whales may mate for life.

sei whale (*Balaenoptera borealis*) 60 ft.

SHEPHERD'S BEAKED WHALE—*See* TASMAN BEAKED WHALE.

SHORT-FINNED PILOT WHALE (*Globicephala macrorhynchus*)—An

odontocete of the Delphinidae family. This twenty-two-foot, five-ton oceanic dolphin is similar to the long-finned pilot whale, except that its dorsal fin and flippers are shorter and it has only thirty-six peglike teeth. Its robust body is black, with patches of gray on the chin, on either side of the blowhole, and behind the dorsal fin. Newborns are 4.5 feet long. This whale may dive more than two thousand feet for squid. It lives in groups of ten to thirty, but herds of several hundred have been seen. It ranges from near shore to offshore in tropical and warm temperate waters of both hemispheres.

short-finned pilot whale (*Globicephala macrorhynchus*) 22 ft.

SHORT-SNOUTED DOLPHIN—*See* FRASER'S DOLPHIN.

SHORT-SNOUTED SPINNER DOLPHIN—*See* CLYMENE DOLPHIN.

SKEW BEAKED WHALE—*See* HECTOR'S BEAKED WHALE.

SNUBFIN—*See* IRRAWADDY DOLPHIN.

SOUTHERN BOTTLENOSE WHALE *(Hyperoodon planifrons)*—An

odontocete of the Ziphiidae family. This twenty-five-foot, three-ton beaked whale is seldom seen and is known mostly from stranded specimens. Males have two teeth located at the tip of the lower jaw. This whale has a beak similar to that of the bottlenose dolphin, quite large flukes, a hooked fifteen-inch fin, and a high, bulbous forehead. The back is metallic gray, shading to paler gray on the sides. There are white spots on the pale belly and throat. The flippers and underside of the flukes are brown. Newborns are nine feet long. The southern bottlenose whale lives in all oceans of the southern hemisphere and may migrate from polar feeding areas to the tropics for calving. It eats squid.

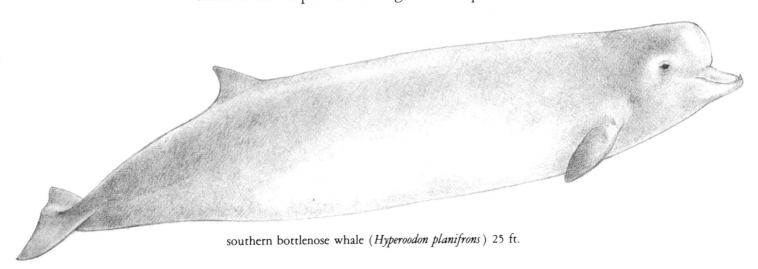

southern bottlenose whale (*Hyperoodon planifrons*) 25 ft.

SOUTHERN FOURTOOTHED WHALE—*See* ARNOUX'S BEAKED WHALE.

SOUTHERN RIGHT WHALE—*See* RIGHT WHALE.

SOUTHERN RIGHT WHALE DOLPHIN *(Lissodelphis peronii)*

—An odontocete of the Delphinidae family. Like the northern right whale dolphin, this six foot, 132-pound oceanic dolphin has no dorsal fin. But unlike the slender northern species, it has a very wide body. The stout beak is very short, and the lower jaw extends past the tip of the upper jaw. This dolphin has 188 tiny, sharp teeth. The hooked flippers are white with a dark rear edge. The belly, snout, sides, and the underside of the deeply notched flukes are white. The back is black. Nothing is known about the young. This dolphin is not well known but has been found in deep offshore waters of South Africa and New Zealand and in coastal waters off Chile. It probably lives throughout the southern oceans. This fast swimmer eats fish and squid.

southern right whale dolphin (*Lissodelphis peronii*) 6 ft.

SOWERBY'S BEAKED WHALE *(Mesoplodon bidens)*—Also called North Sea beaked whale. An odontocete of the Ziphiidae family. This seventeen-foot, three-thousand-pound whale has a sleek body. The forehead slopes steeply to a long, slim beak. Males have two sharply pointed four-inch teeth in the middle of the lower jaw that are visible when the mouth is closed. This whale has a small, hooked dorsal fin just behind midback; short, narrow flippers; flipper pockets; and unnotched flukes. It is dark charcoal gray with a lighter belly and light spots placed irregularly over the body. Newborns are sixty-two inches long. Sowerby's beaked whale lives only in deep temperate to sub-Arctic waters of the North Atlantic. It eats squid and small fish.

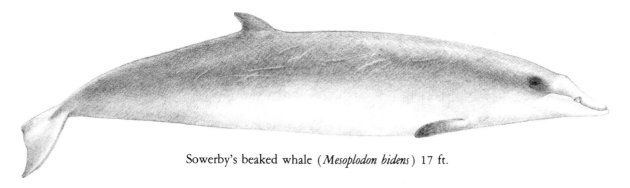

Sowerby's beaked whale (*Mesoplodon bidens*) 17 ft.

SPECTACLED PORPOISE *(Phocoena dioptrica)*—An odontocete of the Phocoenidae family. This 5.5-foot, 110-pound porpoise is similar in shape to the harbor porpoise. It has eighty-four spade-shaped teeth, relatively small flippers set far forward, and a very large triangular dorsal fin. The small, deeply notched flukes are black on top and white on the bottom. The flippers are white with a gray border. The upper half of the body is black, the lower half white. There is a white ring around each eye, and the lips are black. Newborns are a little over 1.5 feet long. This porpoise is rarely seen alive. It lives in cold waters near New Zealand and the tip of South America. It eats squid and fish.

spectacled porpoise *(Phocoena dioptrica)* 5.5 ft.

SPERM WHALE *(Physeter macrocephalus)*—An odontocete of the Physeteridae family. This sixty-foot, sixty-ton whale is the largest of the toothed whales and the only great whale with teeth. It is probably the most familiar whale; it is also the most unusual. Its twelve-ton nose is the largest on record. Unlike any other living whale, it has a single S-shaped blowhole located on the tip of its snout, slightly to the left of center. The bushy

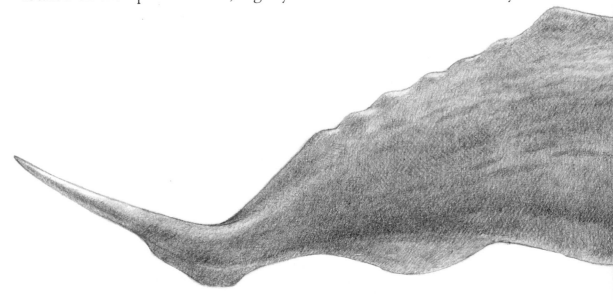

sixteen-foot spout slants forward and to the left. The whale's huge, box-like head is about one-third the length of its entire body. Fifty thick, conical eleven-inch teeth line the underslung lower jaw and fit into sockets in the toothless upper jaw. The huge forehead holds an enormous amount of oil, which may help give the whale neutral buoyancy in deep dives and may allow it to focus strong sonic waves to stun prey. The sperm whale's twenty-pound brain is the largest brain on earth. Instead of a dorsal fin, this whale has a triangular dorsal hump and six-foot-long knuckles along the rear part of the spine. The flippers are short and stubby. The broad, deeply notched sixteen-foot flukes are triangular with a straight rear edge. The fourteen-inch-thick skin of this dark gray whale is the thickest known in the animal kingdom. It sometimes looks wrinkled and is heavily scarred. Newborns are thirteen feet long. Sperm whales live in pods of several females led by one bull. The leader fights fiercely for his females. They inhabit all oceans of the world, from the Arctic to the Antarctic. Most live on the edge of the continental shelf in very deep temperate and tropical waters. Males migrate to cold polar waters. A sperm whale eats eight hundred pounds of squid, octopus, and fish per day. These whales are especially fond of giant squid and sometimes dive thirty-five hundred feet or more to get them. These champion divers can remain underwater for more than an hour and may go as deep as ten thousand feet. Ambergris (AM-ber-grees)—a waxy substance that forms around squid beaks—is sometimes found in their intestines. This valuable substance was once used in making perfume. These whales have been heavily hunted but are now protected in most of their range.

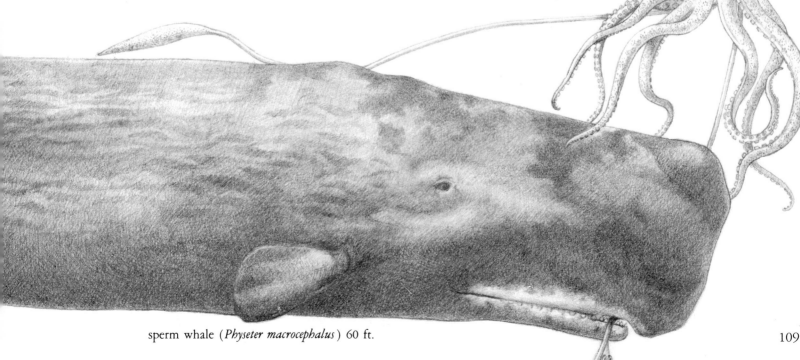

sperm whale (*Physeter macrocephalus*) 60 ft.

SPERM WHALES—*See* PHYSETERIDAE.

SPINNER DOLPHIN *(Stenella longirostris)*—Also called long-snouted spinner dolphin. An odontocete of the Delphinidae family. This graceful, slender-bodied seven-foot, 165-pound oceanic dolphin has 240 small pointed teeth in its long, slender beak—more teeth than any other cetacean. The tall dorsal fin is slightly hooked and in some individuals hooks forward. This dolphin has large, pointed flippers. It is dark gray to black on the back, tan to yellowish brown on the sides, and white on the belly. Some are faintly speckled. Newborns are thirty inches long. There are several varieties of spinner dolphins. They live in large herds in all warm temperate and tropical coastal waters of the world. This acrobatic dolphin frequently leaps clear of the surface and spins on its axis six or seven times. The reason for this behavior is unknown, but it may be a form of communication. Spinner dolphins eat small fish and squid.

spinner dolphins (*Stenella longirostris*) 7 ft.

SPLAYTOOTH BEAKED WHALE—*See* ANDREW'S BEAKED WHALE.

SPOTTED DOLPHIN—*See* BRIDLED SPOTTED DOLPHIN.

SPOTTER DOLPHIN—*See* ATLANTIC SPOTTED DOLPHIN.

SPRAY PORPOISE—*See* DALL'S PORPOISE.

STEJNEGER'S BEAKED WHALE *(Mesoplodon stejnegeri)*—Also

called Bering Sea beaked whale and saber-toothed beaked whale. An odontocete of the Ziphiidae family. Very few of these sixteen-foot beaked whales have ever been seen alive. Males have two massive, protruding five-inch teeth on a ridge in the middle of the lower jaw. This whale has unnotched flukes, rounded flippers, and a moderately large, hooked dorsal fin. Its back is grayish brown; its belly is lighter. Males are covered with scars, presumably inflicted by the teeth of others. Stejneger's beaked whale lives in deep, cold temperate and Arctic waters of the North Pacific and Bering Sea. It eats squid and salmon. There is no information on newborns.

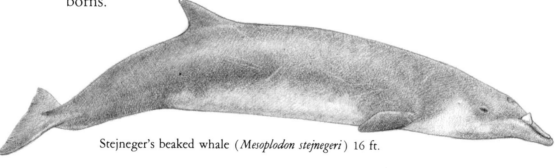

Stejneger's beaked whale (*Mesoplodon stejnegeri*) 16 ft.

STRAP-TOOTHED WHALE *(Mesoplodon layardii)*—An odontocete of

the Ziphiidae family. This seventeen-foot, 2,750-pound whale is among the oddest of the beaked whales. Its long slender beak holds two fourteen-inch-long, two-inch-wide teeth set far back from the tip of the lower jaw. These strange rib-shaped teeth almost meet across the beak, so that the mouth can be opened only a tiny crack. This whale eats squid, which it sucks into its mouth. The small head has a long sloping forehead. The dorsal fin and flippers are also small. The back is dark gray, shading to white on the belly, around the face, and behind the flippers. Newborn calves are seven feet long. This whale lives in all cold, deep waters of the southern hemisphere.

strap-toothed whale (*Mesoplodon layardii*) 17 ft.

STRIPED DOLPHIN *(Stenella coeruleoalba)*—An odontocete of the Delphinidae family. This robust nine-foot, 220-pound oceanic dolphin has a prominent pattern of dark stripes on a grayish background. The throat and belly are white. The beak and flippers are black. The forehead slopes smoothly to a long bottlenose beak lined with two hundred tiny, short, slightly curved teeth. The tall, hooked dorsal fin, tapering flippers, and notched flukes are typical of dolphins. Large herds of several hundred, or even several thousand, live in all temperate to tropical waters of the world, migrating in winter toward the coast or to warmer waters to calve. Newborns are 3.25 feet long. These dolphins eat squid and shrimp. Many are killed in tuna nets.

striped dolphin (*Stenella coeruleoalba*) 9 ft.

striped dolphin calf

SULPHUR BOTTOM WHALE—*See* BLUE WHALE.

SUSU—*See* GANGES RIVER DOLPHIN and INDUS RIVER DOLPHIN.

TASMAN BEAKED WHALE *(Tasmacetus shepherdi)*—Also called Shepherd's beaked whale. An odontocete of the Ziphiidae family. This rare twenty-two-foot, five-thousand-pound beaked whale has never been seen alive and is known only from carcasses. The body is robust, the forehead is rounded, and the beak is long and narrow. The Tasman beaked whale has a small, moderately hooked dorsal fin; short, narrow flippers; and unnotched flukes. Unlike those of most other beaked whales, its upper and lower jaws are lined with many small, conical teeth. In addition, males have two much larger (1.5-inch) teeth located at the tip of the lower jaw. The color of this whale is not definitely known. The back is thought to be darker than the belly. The Tasman beaked whale lives in temperate waters of the southern hemisphere, mostly around New Zealand but also near Chile and Argentina. Stomach contents of carcasses show that it eats fish and squid.

Tasman beaked whale (*Tasmacetus shepherdi*) 22 ft.

TOOTHED WHALES—*See* ODONTOCETI.

TROPICAL WHALE—*See* BRYDE'S WHALE.

TRUE'S BEAKED WHALE *(Mesoplodon mirus)*—An odontocete of the Ziphiidae family. This seventeen-foot, 1.5-ton whale is known only from stranded specimens. The body is chunky at the center and tapers sharply to the tail. The head is small, with a slightly bulging forehead and a distinct beak. Males have two protruding, forward-slanting teeth, triangular in shape and two inches long, set two inches from the tip of the lower jaw. The small flippers are set far forward and unusually low on the body. The flukes are slightly notched. The back is dull black to dark gray, shading to light gray on the belly. Newborns are six feet long. This whale lives in temperate waters of the open sea in the North Atlantic and along the southeast coast of Africa. It probably eats squid.

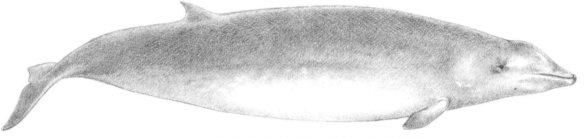

True's beaked whale (*Mesoplodon mirus*) 17 ft.

TUCUXI DOLPHIN *(Sotalia fluviatilis)*—Also called estuarine dolphin. An odontocete of the Delphinidae family. This 4.5-foot, 80-pound oceanic dolphin is one of the smallest dolphins. It is also one of the least known. The tucuxi (tah-KOO-see) dolphin lives in muddy waters and is seldom seen. It has a gently rounding forehead; a curved beak similar to a duck's; 140 small, sharp teeth; a nearly triangular fin; deeply notched flukes; and large, bladelike flippers. Its color varies from blackish brown to gray. The back is generally dark and the belly light. The tucuxi dolphin lives in family groups with strong social ties and stays within a limited home range. It inhabits rivers, flooded jungles, and near-shore marine waters of southeast South America and eastern Central America. It seems to be able to move freely between fresh water and saltwater. It eats fish, prawns, crab, and armored catfish. This unusual dolphin crushes its food before swallowing it.

tucuxi dolphin (*Sotalia fluviatilis*) 4.5 ft.

UNICORN WHALE—*See* NARWHAL.

VAQUITA—*See* GULF PORPOISE.

WEST AFRICAN HUMPBACK DOLPHIN—*See* ATLANTIC HUMP-BACKED DOLPHIN.

WHITE-BEAKED DOLPHIN *(Lagenorhynchus albirostris)*—An odontocete of the Delphinidae family. This ten-foot, 450-pound oceanic dolphin has 112 teeth. Its forehead slopes gently to its two-inch beak. It has a tall, hooked dorsal fin; broad, curving flippers; and shallowly notched flukes. Its back is dark gray to black, with gray patches on the sides and behind the fin. The belly and beak are white to light gray. Newborns are four feet long. This shy, powerful swimmer lives offshore in cold temperate waters of the North Atlantic and is the only dolphin found in the North Atlantic. It is common, sometimes in herds of several hundred, around Iceland. It eats squid, octopus, crustaceans, and fish.

white-beaked dolphin (*Lagenorhynchus albirostris*) 10 ft.

WHITE-STRIPED DOLPHIN—*See* PACIFIC WHITE-SIDED DOLPHIN.

WHITE WHALE—*See* BELUGA.

WHITE WHALES—*See* MONODONTIDAE.

YANGTZE RIVER DOLPHIN—*See* CHINESE RIVER DOLPHIN.

ZIPHIIDAE (Beaked Whales)—A family of toothed whales. There are eighteen species of beaked whales. These are the least known of all whales—in fact, of all large mammals. They live in deep midocean waters and are seldom seen. Some have never been seen alive. These deep-divers have long, narrow snouts or beaks. Their teeth are the most unusual in the animal kingdom. In some species only males have teeth that come through the gums, and in these males, only one or two pairs of teeth erupt in the lower jaw. In other species, both males and females cut teeth. Beaked whales have slender bodies, two throat pleats, crescent-shaped blowholes, and small, backward-sloping fins. The small, triangular dorsal fin sits far behind midback. The wide flukes have either no notch or a very small one. These whales range in size from twelve to forty feet. Most are black or grayish, and males are covered with scratches probably inflicted by the teeth of others when dueling for mates. Beaked whales live in all oceans of the world. They eat mostly squid.

Appendices

Whales Listed by Family

MYSTICETI (*Baleen Whales*)

BALAENIDAE (right whales)
   bowhead whale (*Balaena mysticetus*)
   pygmy right whale (*Caperea marginata*)
   right whale (*Eubalaena glacialis*)

BALAENOPTERIDAE (rorqual whales)
   blue whale (*Balaenoptera musculus*)
   Bryde's whale (*Balaenoptera edeni*)
   fin whale (*Balaenoptera physalus*)
   humpback whale (*Megaptera novaeangliae*)
   minke whale (*Balaenoptera acutorostrata*)
   sei whale (*Balaenoptera borealis*)

ESCHRICHTIIDAE (gray whales)
   gray whale (*Eschrichtius robustus*)

ODONTOCETI (*Toothed Whales*)

DELPHINIDAE (oceanic dolphins)
   Atlantic hump-backed dolphin (*Sousa teuszii*)
   Atlantic spotted dolphin (*Stenella plagiodon*)
   Atlantic white-sided dolphin (*Lagenorhynchus acutus*)
   black dolphin (*Cephalorhynchus eutropia*)

bottlenose dolphin (*Tursiops truncatus*)
bridled spotted dolphin (*Stenella attenuata*)
Clymene dolphin (*Stenella clymene*)
Commerson's dolphin (*Cephalorhynchus commersonii*)
common dolphin (*Delphinus delphis*)
dusky dolphin (*Lagenorhynchus obscurus*)
false killer whale (*Pseudorca crassidens*)
Fraser's dolphin (*Lagenodelphis hosei*)
Heaviside's dolphin (*Cephalorhynchus heavisidii*)
Hector's dolphin (*Cephalorhynchus hectori*)
hourglass dolphin (*Lagenorhynchus cruciger*)
Indo-Pacific hump-backed dolphin (*Sousa chinensis*)
Irrawaddy dolphin (*Orcaella brevirostris*)
killer whale (*Orcinus orca*)
long-finned pilot whale (*Globicephala melaena*)
melon-headed whale (*Peponocephala electra*)
northern right whale dolphin (*Lissodelphis borealis*)
Pacific white-sided dolphin (*Lagenorhynchus obliquidens*)
Peale's dolphin (*Lagenorhynchus australis*)
pygmy killer whale (*Feresa attenuata*)
Risso's dolphin (*Grampus griseus*)
rough-toothed dolphin (*Steno bredanensis*)
short-finned pilot whale (*Globicephala macrorhynchus*)
southern right whale dolphin (*Lissodelphis peronii*)
spinner dolphin (*Stenella longirostris*)
striped dolphin (*Stenella coeruleoalba*)
tucuxi dolphin (*Sotalia fluviatilis*)
white-beaked dolphin (*Lagenorhynchus albirostris*)

MONODONTIDAE (white whales)
beluga (*Delphinapterus leucas*)
narwhal (*Monodon monoceros*)

PHOCOENIDAE (porpoises)
Burmeister's porpoise (*Phocoena spinipinnis*)
Dall's porpoise (*Phocoenoides dalli*)

finless porpoise (*Neophocaena phocaenoides*)
gulf porpoise (*Phocoena sinus*)
harbor porpoise (*Phocoena phocoena*)
spectacled porpoise (*Phocoena dioptrica*)

PHYSETERIDAE (sperm whales)
dwarf sperm whale (*Kogia simus*)
pygmy sperm whale (*Kogia breviceps*)
sperm whale (*Physeter macrocephalus*)

PLATANISTIDAE (river dolphins)
Amazon River dolphin (*Inia geoffrensis*)
Chinese river dolphin (*Lipotes vexillifer*)
franciscana dolphin (*Pontoporia blainvillei*)
Ganges River dolphin (*Platanista gangetica*)
Indus River dolphin (*Platanista minor*)

ZIPHIIDAE (beaked whales)
Andrew's beaked whale (*Mesoplodon bowdoini*)
Arnoux's beaked whale (*Berardius arnuxii*)
Baird's beaked whale (*Berardius bairdii*)
Blainville's beaked whale (*Mesoplodon densirostris*)
Cuvier's beaked whale (*Ziphius cavirostris*)
ginkgo-toothed beaked whale (*Mesoplodon ginkgodens*)
Gray's beaked whale (*Mesoplodon grayi*)
Gulf Stream beaked whale (*Mesoplodon europaeus*)
Hector's beaked whale (*Mesoplodon hectori*)
Hubbs' beaked whale (*Mesoplodon carlhubbsi*)
Indo-Pacific beaked whale (*Mesoplodon pacificus*)
northern bottlenose whale (*Hyperoodon ampullatus*)
southern bottlenose whale (*Hyperoodon planifrons*)
Sowerby's beaked whale (*Mesoplodon bidens*)
Stejneger's beaked whale (*Mesoplodon stejnegeri*)
strap-toothed whale (*Mesoplodon layardii*)
Tasman beaked whale (*Tasmacetus shepherdi*)
True's beaked whale (*Mesoplodon mirus*)

For Further Reading

BUNTING, EVE. *The Seaworld Book of Whales*. New York: Harcourt Brace Jovanovich, 1980.

CALDWELL, MELBA C., and CALDWELL, DAVID K. "Communication in Atlantic Bottlenosed Dolphins." *Sea Frontiers,* May 1979, pp. 130–39.

CONLY, ROBERT L. "Porpoises, Our Friends at Sea." *National Geographic,* September 1966, pp. 396–425.

COUSTEAU, JACQUES-YVES, and DIOLE, PHILLIPPE. *Whales: Monarchs of the Sea*. Garden City, New York: Doubleday and Co., 1972.

DARLING, JIM. "Source of the Humpback's Song." *Oceans,* March/April 1984, pp. 3–10.

ELLIS, RICHARD. *The Book of Whales*. New York: Alfred A. Knopf, Inc., 1980.

GARDNER, ROBERT. *The Whale Watcher's Guide*. New York: Messner, 1984.

GIDDINGS, AL. "An Incredible Feasting of Whales." *National Geographic,* January 1984, pp. 88–93.

GORMLEY, GERARD. "Hungry Humpbacks Forever Blowing Bubbles." *Sea Frontiers,* September/October 1983, pp. 258–65.

HOYT, ERICH. "The Whales Called Killer." *National Geographic,* August 1984, pp. 220–37.

LEATHERWOOD, STEPHEN, and REEVES, RANDALL R. *The Sierra Club Handbook of Whales and Dolphins*. San Francisco: Sierra Club Books, 1983.

McGOWEN, TOM. *Album of Whales*. Chicago: Rand McNally & Company, 1980.

MINASIAN, STANLEY M., and BALCOMB, KENNETH C. III. *The World's Whales.* Washington, D.C.: Smithsonian Books, 1984.

OLIVER, JOHN. "Strip Mining on the Pacific Floor Where the Gray Whale Feeds." *Oceans,* March 1983, p. 16.

PAYNE, ROGER. "At Home with the Right Whales." *National Geographic,* March 1976, pp. 322–39.

SCHEFFER, VICTOR. "The Cliche of the Killer Whale." *Natural History,* October 1970, pp. 26–28.

SLIJPER, EVERHARD. *Whales and Dolphins.* Ann Arbor, Michigan: The University of Michigan Press, 1976.

VIETMEYER, NOEL D. "Rare Narwhals Inspired the Myth of the Unicorn." *Smithsonian,* February 1980, pp. 118–24.

WALKER, THEODORE J. *Whale Primer.* Washington, D.C.: Cabrillo Historical Association, 1979.

WATSON, LYALL. *Sea Guide to Whales of the World.* New York: E. P. Dutton, 1981.

WHITEHEAD, HAL. "The Unknown Giants/Sperm and Blue Whales." *National Geographic,* December 1984, pp. 774–89.

————. "Why Whales Leap." *Scientific American,* March 1985, pp. 84–93.

WISE, TERENCE. *Whales and Dolphins.* Milwaukee: Raintree Children's Books, 1980.

WÜRSIG, BERND. "Dolphins." *Scientific American,* March 1979, pp. 136–48.

Index

HELEN RONEY SATTLER was born in Iowa and graduated cum laude from Southwest Missouri State College with a B.S. in education. She taught elementary school for nine years and was a children's librarian for one year. She began writing stories for her son when he was small; later, immobilized by a back injury and "not being able to lie there doing nothing," she wrote several stories that she sold to magazines. "Since nothing succeeds like success," she says, "I've been at it ever since."

Ms. Sattler's early books for Lothrop include *Train Whistles* and *Recipes for Art and Craft Materials,* both popular books that have been reissued in updated editions. Her grandson's fascination with dinosaurs, and the inadequate materials available for young readers, suggested a direction for her work that has established her as a leading science writer for children. *Dinosaurs of North America* was a Golden Kite Honor Book, an ALA Notable Book, and a Boston Globe–Horn Book Honor Book; *The Illustrated Dinosaur Dictionary* won a Golden Kite Award; *Pterosaurs, the Flying Reptiles, Baby Dinosaurs,* and *Sharks, the Super Fish,* like their predecessors, have been warmly praised by reviewers.

Ms. Sattler has traveled widely to do research for her books. She lives with her husband in Bartlesville, OK.

JEAN DAY ZALLINGER has been drawing pictures since she can remember. She was born and raised in Massachusetts and received a Bachelor of Fine Arts degree from the Yale School of Fine Arts. She has illustrated over fifty books for children, including *Baby Dinosaurs* by Helen Roney Sattler. Her pictures for Ms. Sattler's previous book, *Sharks, the Super Fish,* were called "distinguished" by ALA *Booklist,* "attractive and informative" by *The Horn Book,* and "glorious and accurate" by *School Library Journal.* Ms. Zallinger lives in Connecticut and is Professor Emeritus of illustration and drawing at the Paier College of Art.